D0941921

Washington Public Library

DISCARD

THE CRUCIAL TASK OF THEOLOGY

E. ASHBY JOHNSON

The CRUCIAL TASK *of* THEOLOGY

John Knox Press
RICHMOND, VIRGINIA

Whitworth College Library
Spokane, Washington

Library of Congress Catalog Card Number: 58-7773

Copyright © 1958 by C. D. Deans, Richmond, Virginia
Printed in the United States of America
5490

51,796

To

my WIFE

With appreciation

and love

FOREWORD

Time was when *the* "crucial task of theology" was to get either the pious or the thoughtful to take it seriously. The story is told of the great church historian, Adolf Harnack, that when he was moving from one house to another nearby he enlisted some of his students to help transport his books. In the new house, the boys were re-shelving them and came to a pile of books in theology. "Where do these go?" they asked the master. "Oh, those," he replied with a shrug. "Put them alongside the other belles-lettres!"

This sort of thing used to seem deliciously funny to a generation taught by both pietism and its rationalistic opposite that theology was more of an intellectual game than a serious business—far inferior to "religious experience" if it was an affair of the heart; equally inferior to philosophy (or science) if it was an affair of the head. From Schleiermacher's time down to D. C. MacIntosh the theologian had to begin with a justification of his project.

It is a commonplace that theology has made a comeback in these latter days. In many quarters, indeed, it has become almost fashionable! More people nowadays could name three or four outstanding theologians—and be right about it—than could list the same number of front-rank philosophers. Seminary courses in theology are elected far beyond the required

7

minimum. Ministers and laymen are reading more serious—
and more interesting!—books in theology than ever in living
memory. And books there are, in gracious plenty, for *almost*
every level and angle of theological thought.

And yet, if the theological neophyte should ask—most reasonably—for an "introduction" to theology *as a distinctive
method of human inquiry,* the fact leaps up that there is a
curious shortage at just this point. Theological books still
have their "prolegomena." There is a vast library on "the
problem of religious knowledge." And every theological system has a hermeneutical principle, expressed or implied. But
none of these serves to survey theology as an intellectual discipline or to define theology's scope, aims, and limitations in
the face of the multiplicity of theological types. Every discipline has its characteristic "field" and general procedure, and
one of the elementary tasks in mastering a field is to understand its typical ways of working. Every theological teacher
often wishes for an adequate "introduction" to put into his
students' hands; for he knows that even a faithful study of
theology which lacks critical perspective will end either in
general bafflement or with an accidental set of partisan biases.

The chief virtue of Professor Johnson's book is that it
affords just such a needed guide to the study and practice of
theology. It is an interesting and competent analysis of how
theological notions are framed and how they may be ap-
praised; it analyzes the alternative presuppositions which
shape and direct theological discussion and shows how these
effect the end product; it explores the correlations between
theology on the one hand and philosophy and modern science
on the other; it ventures into the fascinating territory of "the
symbolic presentation of non-propositional truth." It gives
an instructive picture of a theologian at work—dealing forth-
rightly with the questions which arise at the very outset of the

theological enterprise and which affect the whole process of inquiry and statement. And these questions deserve responsible consideration by all who propose to talk about religion at all, whether from within faith's sanctuary or from "the seat of the scornful." *The* crucial task of theology, in Professor Johnson's mind, is to make clear what it is all about. And this he has done, in most helpful fashion.

Beyond the students and ministers who need such an introduction to theology, there are two other groups which ought especially to profit from it. The one is those who are going to theologize anyway—even with due disclaimers—when they undertake to explain the Christian message to an uncomprehending mind. These theologians in spite of themselves need to understand what it is they are doing—and learn how to do it more responsibly. The other group who need to revise their unexamined prejudice against theology are the modern intellectuals who take it for granted that theology is, by nature, a form of special pleading and hence cannot be intellectually respectable. This suspicion is often coupled with another: that theology is incurably sectarian and polemic. The two suspicions lead to the same conclusion: theology is the indoor sport of the doctrinaire.

Both these detractors of theology might very well learn from this book that theology is a rigorous and rational affair which has distinctive methods and problems but shares the common logic of all critical inquiry. The fideists can learn that there are norms for testing the cogency of a theological notion which transcend the intensity of personal feeling or the weight of external authority. The secularists can discover here that the good theologian is in vital conversation with his fellow inquirers in other fields and deserves a respectful hearing in the open forum of the intellectual community. If more people knew more clearly what theology really is—and is up to—the theological revival would gain substance and depth in the contemporary scene.

There are three significant emphases in this book which are worthy of mention in a foreword. The first is the unusually broad scope of Dr. Johnson's conception of theology. He is sensitive to the variety and clash of theological systems—and he has no desire to relax the tension between competing views. But he takes pains to see—and to show his reader—the positive values of each of the contenders, and so fends off the temptation to premature and one-sided conclusions. The author happens to be a Presbyterian; I *think* I could have deduced it from the text even if I hadn't already known it. But I did not find a single instance where an argument was skewed to fit a bias. In this sense, the book has been conceived and written in the true ecumenical spirit.

A second point to be commended is the attention paid here to the bearing of modern logic and linguistic analysis upon the old problems of meaning and verification for theological propositions. This is an exciting new development which has not been fully appreciated by theologians of the old school. Johnson is very much alive to its import for theological method, and turns it to positive account. Indeed, his own conception of "convergence as the integrating method of theology" is worth noting as a good sample of the use to which these newer analytic tools can be put.

A third item that will interest the reader, I think, is Johnson's notion of what he calls "hairetic judgment." This may turn out to be a good deal more than a startling and awkward coinage. One of the pressing issues in theology is the status of judgments which turn, in the last analysis, upon inaccessible and private forces deep inside the subject-self. Some theologians propose to make a virtue of this necessity, by affecting to despise "objectivity" and by exalting irrational notions of "decision," "engagement," and the like. Johnson faces this whole vexed problem steadily, and steadily refuses to settle for a plausible extreme. And, in the process, he has come up with an interpretation of the role of personal decision in the formation of theological judgments which makes a lot of sense.

As a theological educator, my main concern with this book is the fact that it goes far toward meeting an urgent need in certain basic courses in the theological curriculum. And what helps here will be of value to the minister and thoughtful layman as well. They will appreciate its relaxed and readable style and the way the author's sprightly and irenic temper shines through his earnest argumentation. The student who gets his methodological orientation in these pages will be well prepared for the further tasks that lie beyond. This is a book to be used and chewed. It won't be shelved as belles-lettres.

Albert C. Outler
Perkins School of Theology
Southern Methodist University
Dallas, Texas

PREFACE

Theology is characterized by its willingness to ask "big questions." When I find myself growing impatient with the apparent tendency on the part of writers in the field of religion to rely upon rhetoric and obscurity as a substitute for rigorous thought, I quickly return to a realization that this tendency is an evidence not of evasiveness on the part of the writer but of the magnitude of the subject matter. In trivial and inconsequential matters it is possible to be extremely clear and precise. It is possible to preserve this rigor in thought if one simply refuses to ask any questions which do not lend themselves to simple answers. Theology, however, cannot accept this easy way out. It must presume to deal with matters of ultimate reality and meaning. In its ambitious endeavor it exposes itself to the charge of vagueness and lack of precision.

During the past century the dominant feature of Western thought has been its analytic rather than synthetic orientation. Ever since Kant the epistemological question has tended to take priority over the ontological question. Method has precedence over content; we are asking *how* we know rather than *what* we know. Science has come to be identified with a form of procedure rather than with any set of conclusions.

Philosophy has concerned itself with the critical examination of the means of empirical and rational investigation rather than with the production of comprehensive systems.

If theology is to commend itself to an age of analysis, it must share in some measure in this methodological concern. Even at the risk of discovering weaknesses in its own approach, theology must examine and define its procedure and criteria. Only by a description of its own methodology and a faithful adherence to it can theology win a hearing from an age which is seriously concerned with method.

In this interest I have undertaken an examination of theological aims and procedure. This book is, of course, written as an expression of a need on my own part to work through my thinking on the subject. It is written also in the hope of stimulating further inquiry into theological method, not simply as an apology for existing theological conclusions, but as an open examination of the form of vindication to which theology may properly appeal.

I wish to express my deep appreciation to the Board of Christian Education of the Presbyterian Church, U.S. for the Fellowship which provided me with the opportunity for a year of research at Yale University in the preparation of this work. I am genuinely grateful to King College for a year's leave of absence and to Austin College for the lightening of certain duties during the revision of the manuscript. I acknowledge my indebtedness to William A. Christian of Yale University and to Frank Bell Lewis of Union Theological Seminary in Virginia for their reading and many helpful suggestions in the preparation of this book. I express my sincere appreciation to my wife for her encouragement and for her patient reading of the manuscript and careful correction of errors.

CONTENTS

Whitworth College Library
Spokane, Washington

Christian theology in the twentieth century has been called upon to justify its existence. Sincere adherents to the Christian faith denounce as impious rationalism all human efforts to inquire into the nature and work of God. Equally sincere secular philosophers, armed with a clearly specified analytic method, deny the possibility of making any sensible statements regarding transcendent reality. If theology is to retain its place among the serious activities of men, it must be prepared to meet these criticisms.

The most effective answer which theology can give takes the form of an examination and clear statement of its approach and method. It must indicate the subject matter with which it is prepared to deal, the manner in which it proposes to conduct its inquiry, the tests to which its statements may be subjected, and the form in which it finds it possible to communicate its findings. This is the crucial task of theology.

THE CONTEMPORARY
CHALLENGE TO THEOLOGY

SLIGHTLY more than a century ago Auguste Comte pronounced the sentence of death upon theology: his confident prediction that in all its expressions theology is an anachronism destined soon to disappear from the area of serious human activities. Within the neat framework of his rather superficial philosophy of history he viewed a theological interpretation of life as characteristic of the primitive and infantile stage of human development. In the childhood of the race man had no real understanding of the world in which he lived and in his ignorance turned to mythological and supernaturalistic explanations of the forces which he encountered. He viewed the phenomena of existence as an expression of arbitrary forces whose nature must remain a mystery and whose favorable activity could best be assured through religious cultic practices. Having constructed mythological explanations and religious institutions to perpetuate them, immature man proceeded to believe his own fairytales and to subject himself to the traditional authorities which they engendered.

Even as the human individual grows from childhood into adolescence, so, according to Comte, the race progresses from the theological age into the metaphysical. In the advance of civilization, man developed to the point where he became conscious of possessing the critical faculties of rationality and discernment. In the exercise of these faculties he came to detect the glaring inconsistencies and radical absurdities of his childish fancies and to reject as inadequate his theological formulations. The same rational powers which revealed the falseness of the mythological view of the world seemed to promise a new way of understanding, that of metaphysical speculation. In that stage man rejoiced in his new-found powers and constructed systems of abstract philosophy characterized by ingenuity rather than clarity. As man had once been enslaved by his fear and credulity, he now became victim of his own vague subtleties. The adolescent flights of fancy produced intricate spiderwebs of abstract reasoning but, like the earlier theological interpretations, provided no realistic understanding of man or of the world in which he lived.

Comte concluded that the signs of genuine maturity of the race began to appear when man, putting away the childish things of mythology and discovering the futility of metaphysical speculation, came to rely upon the inductive methodology of natural science to provide him with dependable knowledge of the world and with the power which such knowledge assured. Comte viewed with unrestrained optimism the picture of mankind standing at the threshold of the new age, the age of positivism, when facts, carefully observed and measured, would supplant tradition and speculation as the sure groundwork of truth. Although vestigial traces of theology and philosophy still exist among the unenlightened, these activities, having outlived their usefulness, must gradually cease, and the institutions which they have produced must either crumble or undergo radical reconstruction at the hands of science.

Not all of Comte's condescending assumptions have been vindicated by the events of the past century. His requiem for metaphysics and theology was distinctly premature; both these forms of activity have demonstrated a remarkable vitality and a perverse reluctance to lie down quietly and expire on schedule. The widespread conviction of the mid-nineteenth century regarding the utter exhaustion of religious and metaphysical resources seems ridiculously naïve in the light of subsequent development.

The spectacular advances of natural science, confidently anticipated by Comte, have not resulted in the disappearance of the need for metaphysical speculation but rather in an increased demand for rationalistic generalization. The process of scientific investigation is not the simple accumulation of observations which Francis Bacon supposed it to be, nor are the generalizations of science accomplished apart from speculative outreach. Metaphysical inquiry is of the very essence of contemporary science. The conceptualizations necessary to modern research cannot be proposed apart from basic metaphysical presuppositions and lend themselves only to mathematical presentation.[1] Simple mechanistic explanation of the physical universe has, perforce, given way to speculative constructions which break down any supposed division between physics and metaphysics. It is certainly true that only at his peril can the metaphysician ignore the results of observational science, but it is equally true that science finds itself in the position not of supplanting philosophical speculation but of placing increased reliance upon it.

Comparably, the evidence of the past century does not point to any withering away of theological concern and activity. One needs only to glance over the literature, scholarly and popular, of the past few generations in order to be convinced that the increase of scientific knowledge has entailed no diminution of the felt relevance of a religious interpretation of life. The "religious revival" which has been such an obvious aspect of the mid-twentieth century scene, although it has many superficial features, is characterized by theological resurgence. Seldom within the history of the Church has there been a time when evangelistic fervor has been accompanied by and undergirded with such creative theological activity. Protestant, Roman Catholic, Anglican, Orthodox, and Jewish communities have found worthy champions of their faith, scholars concerned not with resisting the encroachments of science but competent to bring upon the intellectual scene religious interpretations which give full weight to the accomplishments in all fields of human inquiry.

Both metaphysics and theology raise certain questions and propose answers; questions which Comte predicted would either receive positive answer from science or else be demonstrated as inconsequential. There is a certain plausibility to the assumption that the more questions science can answer with empirical verification the less place there is for the speculative outreaches of philosophy and the pronouncements of theology. This apparent supplanting of speculation and religious proclamation by "knowledge" proves, however, to be deceptive. It is not necessary to presume *a priori* that there are specific matters which cannot be brought within the scope of inductive investigation. We need only to recognize that the satisfactory answering of one question does not put an end to curiosity but rather serves to raise additional questions. Similarly, there seem to be certain questions of almost universal concern which are no less significant because of the fact that they have been asked for centuries without producing uniform answers; questions which are of such nature that no additional factual information seems to bring us any closer to a final and conclusive answer but serves only to permit a rephrasing of the question. So far as we can see we are dealing with matters analogous to an infinite mathematical series in which no finite increment brings us significantly closer to a final term. Efforts to answer these questions are not cumulative in the same manner that the body of data employed in the problems of science is cumulative; increase in information may modify the context in which the questions are raised, may also influence the relative weight accorded to particular solutions; but the available knowledge is never adequate for a conclusive judgment.[2]

Success in answering various questions of immediate concern in no degree lessens the intensity or urgency with which man asks the question of ultimate concern. The Alexandrian Greeks asked the question as to the dimensions of the earth and gave a calculated answer which is impressive in its degree of accuracy. Twentieth-century instruments and methods produce an answer in which the margin of error is reduced, in which the information may be taken to be more precise. The anatomists of the Renaissance added greatly to the classical descriptions of the human body and to the understanding of the function of the various organs, even as subsequent physiological studies have produced a growing comprehension of biological structure and function. Questions of this order may be asked, and the knowledge is cumulative, permitting a genuine growth in understanding and accuracy. However, the men of each era have continued to ask, "What is the meaning of my existence on this earth?" and more precise answers to the descriptive problems either of the earth or of man do not serve to provide an answer to the ultimate question or to diminish the urgency with which it is asked. Accordingly, we neither see nor anticipate seeing a diminution of interest in the problems of theology or in the efforts to deal with them.

Although it is not possible to take seriously Comte's "prophecy" of the impending death of metaphysics and theology in the immediate or foreseeable future, he is historically vindicated at one point; "the age of positivism" has called into being a complex conceptual orientation which presents a serious challenge to the past accomplishments and continued functioning of theology. It would be far beyond the evidence to suggest that scientific development has either taken over the role of theology or rendered its activity superfluous. What science as such, together with the reflections upon the nature of the world which it has stimulated, has done, however, is to engender an intellectual climate in which a standard is proposed in terms of which theology finds its competence challenged.

A critical estimate of theology has been aroused both from the Christian community—the Church for which theology proposes to speak—and from the secular world with which it endeavors to communicate. The exact form of the challenge varies greatly, but underlying the criticism from both quarters there is the call for theology to present its credentials, to specify the means by which its conclusions are reached.

The entire discipline of theology—systematic, historical, Biblical, philosophical—is called in question. It is not simply one "school" which is under suspicion but the entire enterprise. Theology has its variety of forms, but in all its expressions it is *that human inquiry which undertakes to present in intelligible form a coherent and comprehensive statement of truths which are of ultimate concern to man.*[3]

It is because theology manifests itself as a *human* enterprise bent upon giving an answer to *human* concerns, and because of its endeavor to commend itself as genuinely comprehensible to the human mind, that it is most frequently brought under indictment from the Christian community. Yet it is in this light that theology must be recognized. Theology is an enterprise of men, and whatever subject matter it may seek to include, its formulations and expressions are the product of human endeavor and are designed to conform to human categories of thought. The *Summa Theologica* and *Institutes of the Christian Religion* were not only written through human effort but also are structured to appeal to characteristic human responses. The fact that in one degree or another they have received the official sanction of significant bodies within the Christian Church and have been accorded normative value in no sense obscures their anthropological orientation. Nor is this limited to so-called "systematics." Exegetical or Biblical theology are of the same order. The exegete and the systematizer are alike engaged in a form of human inquiry which relies upon human discernment and effort.

If it is because of its human involvement that theology is sometimes criticized from within the Church, it is because of its aspiration to be comprehensive, even to the point of ultimate concern, that theology is called upon by the secular world to present its credentials. If it were not endeavoring to make its work both intelligible and convincing, if it did not claim that its findings are *true,* it would meet with no particular protest from the secular world. It is upon the basis of its competence as a way of arriving at what is true that theology is challenged.

In a sense both the secular and the religious world raise the question: "How do you presume to make statements about that which lies beyond human experience, and on what basis are you calling upon us to accept these statements as true?" The religious world may indict theology as impious and proud; the secular world may denounce it as unreliable or absurd. In each case, however, the central matter which is called in question is the *method* by which theology derives its conclusions.

There is nothing new about a situation in which the competence of theology is called in question. Every serious inquiry, by virtue of its claim to assent, subjects itself to serious criticism and can expect to claim assent only as it is prepared to justify its claims. The nature and extent of the indictments of theology are such that they cannot be brushed aside. Since the work of theology anticipates acceptance and is pointless except as directed toward that end, it must undertake to meet all calls upon it to present a clear statement of its procedure and approach.

The Challenge to Theology from Within the Christian Community

Although theology comes into being as a function of the Church and finds its significance only within the framework of the continuing witness of the Church, it is an activity which a part of the Christian community desires to disown or denounce. Theology meets its severest, certainly its most numerous and vocal, critics among those members of its own community who feel that the supernatural character of the Christian revelation is such that it permits no rational investigation or intellectual interpretation. Christian truth is affirmed to be completely foreign to speculative activity or rational analysis; it lies totally within the realm of faith and calls for acceptance rather than inquiry. In the name of faith systematic theology is looked upon with suspicion or is denounced as an evidence of pride and impiety. The content of religious faith is regarded as supernaturally imparted and therefore as calling for no rational vindication and subject to no rational criticism. The possibility of theology as a form of *human inquiry* is categorically denied.

The voices of the Church Fathers were often raised in protest against any tendency to interpret Christianity as a philosophical system or to compromise in any degree its distinctive non-rational character. Tertullian was insistent upon the complete incompatibility of "Athens and Jerusalem," was inflexible in his assertion that no human faculty is competent to interpret, much less to modify in the least degree, the essentially supernatural quality of the Christian message. In the formulative period of the Western Church it was most frequently his point of view which prevailed over the more speculative and rationalistic approach of Origen. The protest of Tertullian was directed primarily not against anti-Christian philosophical systems but against the tendency to introduce philosophical methods and criteria into Christian proclamation. Even after speculative activity had established for itself a role in the Church, Peter Domiani and Anselm endeavored to assure that all such exercise of reason be kept thoroughly subservient to dogmatic considerations. Even at the height of Roman and Protestant Scholasticism there arose sincere and vocal protests against "intellectualized Christianity," the warning of the mystic and the traditionalist that the eye of reason is blind to that which is apprehended only through the eye of faith.

In the present century the denunciation of systematic or philosophical theology is as significant and persistent as at any period of history. This protest in the name of faith comes in large measure from that element of the Christian community which is relatively unsophisticated. It constitutes a challenge by virtue of the number of persons involved, but it is undergirded by little or no genuine understanding either of the work of theology or of the character of the convictions which are defended. Quite frequently this championship of "faith" is an expression of fear rather than of confidence. There exists the lurking suspicion that the articles of belief would not stand the test of critical examination and that, consequently, they are best preserved by demanding that they be kept inviolate from rational inquiry. Even where this fear is not dominant there tends to exist a serious confusion of ideas.

When the protest is raised against the activity of systematic theology, it is in fact nothing more than a protest against *contemporary* systematic theology. Although the fact is not recognized by the adherents, the formulations of some past generation, perhaps in the thirteenth or sixteenth century, are taken to be final and normative. There exists the illusion that these systems, themselves the product of men of past generations, are somehow direct pronouncements of God "untouched by human hands." The effort to keep matters of faith completely distinct from all forms of rational inquiry is not, as supposed, a defense of divine truth from the hands of human definement but, rather, an uncritical loyalty to one body of human construction as over against subsequent efforts of the same order. Only an ignorance of the historical origins of the accepted formulae, obscuring by time of the nature of the heritage, makes possible this artificial disjunction.

While it is true that, simply in terms of the number of people involved, the strength of the contemporary protest against systematic theology in the name of faith is more a matter of ignorance than of understanding, it would be a serious mistake to conclude that the challenge may be ignored as arising *only* from blind prejudice and obscurantism. It is not the ignorant alone who warn against the presumptive exercise of human wisdom in matters of Christian faith. On the present scene there is no dearth of thoughtful and sophisticated scholars who find it justifiable to protest against the usurpation by human reason of an authority it does not rightfully possess, and against the exercise of finite judgment in an area where reason is not competent either to construct or to criticize. Against such critics the countercharge of ignorance would be absurd. Their challenge is based not upon blind devotion but upon the firm conviction that there exists a realm of truth in which human faculties are competent not to investigate but only to receive.

Within the Roman Catholic Church, of course, there has historically existed an effective resistance against all revisionist tendencies on the part of theology. The two dominant movements within modern Catholicism, the Scotist and Thomist strains, have been alike in preserving Christian dogma from revised rationalistic construction. The former strain assents to a form of ecclesiastical positivism which permits no serious investigation of matters concerning which there exist official Church pronouncements. The modern Thomist certainly is no scorner of reason; he preserves the Aquinian respect for both philosophy and revealed truth, but does so only by maintaining a methodological disjunction between them. Metaphysics is to be undertaken in terms of the most rigorous ratio-empirical procedure, but the supernatural truths of the Christian faith are in no sense subject to the same criteria. Thus: "Viewed as a formally constructed philosophy, Thomistic philosophy—I do not say Thomistic theology—is wholly rational: no reasoning issuing from faith finds its way into its inner fabric; it derives intrinsically from reason and rational criticism alone; and its soundness as a philosophy is based entirely on experimental or intellectual evidence and on logical proof."[4] The autonomy of philosophy in the realm of nature is complete and unqualified but, conversely, it has no true function with respect to the supernatural. Theology is not a rational but a recording function. "Theology is not a simple application of philosophy to revealed data—as many have thought since the time of Descartes. Were this so it would involve submitting the content of faith to human judgment and discernment. Theology is a *habitus* of wisdom rooted in faith: hence it is radically and virtually supernatural, and hence it uses philosophical knowledge as its instrument and judges it in its own light. It is so to speak an impression in us of the divine knowledge, and its only specifying object is Deity as such."[5]

It may seem incongruous to suggest that Thomas Aquinas, or the multitude of his followers, with all the systematic accomplishments of the Thomistic movement, should constitute an attack upon the theological enterprise. The methodological disjunction, however, which specifies one approach for philosophy and another for theology effectively removes the latter from the area of human activity. Not only is human reason declared to be incompetent to construct or criticize supernatural knowledge, it is unable even to draw any valid inferences from those items of faith which are held simply *as believed*.[6] That Thomism does assent to an intellectually formulated system of supernatural truth is a fundamental inconsistency.

From within the Protestant branch of Christianity there arises the same indictment of human inquiry in matters of divine truth which has dominated the Roman Church. The fundamentalism which had its ascendancy in the nineteenth century and is still strong in the twentieth would hypostatize a particular body of propositions and demand assent to them without reference either to principles of logic or facts of experience. Such fundamentalism acknowledges no valid criteria for these propositions which are equated with divine truth except the self-authentication of implicit faith.

Although it is the avowed critic of both Catholic authoritarianism and Protestant fundamentalism, the neo-orthodox movement presents its own challenge to systematic theology. In a sense, because it takes with radical seriousness the consequences of the fall of man, neo-orthodoxy would seem to overreach even the "old orthodoxies" in denying to human faculties any reliability in the determination of divine truth.

The whole being of man, not merely his supernatural graces, is seen as corrupt and fragmented. Consequently, there is no possibility that his reason, distorted by sin along with the rest of his being, should afford any means of discerning either the true state of man or his way of escape.

It is possible, of course, to draw certain passages, particularly from the earlier writings of the movement, which could be branded as radical irrationalism. A number of these more extreme statements have been modified or rephrased with the passing of the years in such a manner that much of the emphasis has been tempered. What stands as a protest against a naturalized and rationalized religion need not be taken as an epistemological postulation. DeWolf recognizes that it is only a caricature of neo-orthodoxy to view it as the use of reason to discredit reason. "Irrationalism is, naturally, an irrational trend, not a systematic epistemology."[7] The movement is not anti-intellectual in the sense of rejecting all criteria of judgment in favor of a glorification of sheer absurdity; rather it constitutes a warning against "reason's axiom of the final reality of reason."[8]

The sense in which neo-orthodoxy constitutes a challenge to theology is that it protests against according to any humanly constructed formulation any genuine significance as an adequate vehicle of divine truth. In its concern lest reasonableness be accorded final authority, it suggests that reasonableness does not constitute a valid criterion in the realm of Christian truth. In its protest against system as an end in itself it would seem to discount the instrumental value of systematization. In its caution against the inevitable distortions produced by sin-warped reason it would suggest that for man to rely upon reason as his path to understanding is more than a tragic self-delusion—it is an arrogant denial of his own creatureliness.

Even when neo-orthodoxy is recognized as something other than an exaltation of the irrational it still stands as a challenge that the work of theology, seen as a human enterprise, can lead not to accomplishment but to frustration. There is a necessity for an intelligent and coherent elucidation of the Christian proclamation, and theology is called upon to meet that need. However, the very faculties which man must employ in this task, his experience and reason, are looked upon as unreliable and deceptive. Brunner acknowledges the traditional task of theology, that of a reasonable exposition of Christian truth, as completely justifiable: "For the sake of the Gospel the Church cannot ignore its duty to distinguish false doctrine from true: to this end it must make the effort to express the content of its simple teaching in more exact and thoughtful terms. . . . Hence the Church cannot fail to develop her doctrine in the sense of giving more exact and precise definitions of ideas; then, she must show the connexion of these ideas with the whole body of Christian truth."[9] He contends, however, that there is no faculty which can "pass judgment on the claim of faith or the claim of revelation" and that these claims remain "the act and venture of faith."[10]

It is not difficult to cite passages from Karl Barth which would seem to denounce as impious all rational enterprise in the effort to make Christian truth either lucid or logically consistent. However, he makes it clear that he is quite willing to consider theology as a "science" in the sense that: "1. Like all other so-called sciences, it is a human effort after a definite object of knowledge. 2. Like all other sciences, it follows a definite, self-consistent path of knowledge. 3. Like all other sciences, it is in the position of being accountable for this path to itself and to every one—every one who is capable of effort after this object and therefore of following this path."[11]

His stipulation is that theology can acknowledge no genuine criterion except the *analogia fidei* which overrides all other standards of judgment.[12]

The particular task which Barth assigns to theology, or dogmatics, makes it possible for him to make full exercise of rational criteria and, at the same time, deny final authority to reason. The task of theology is that of examining critically the *language* of the Church, of testing the proclamation which is presented to the world.[13] The point is that theology does not and cannot produce the message which comes from the Church. Its work is not constructive but critical. Neither can it presume to produce a really consistent system: "It absolutely cannot regard itself as a member of an ordered cosmos, but only as a stop-gap in an unordered one."[14] Theology can and should check the language which the Church speaks regarding both its adequacy for the times and its fidelity to the Word of God. In this function it employs the normal faculties of thought and claims no special key to wisdom. These faculties, however, cannot produce, and should not aspire to, a comprehensive and consistent statement of Christian truth.

Systematic theology is subjected to criticism from both the Roman Catholic and Protestant branches of the Church in the form of a warning against the injection of rationalistic criteria into the realm of faith. From another quarter it encounters a challenge in the name of Christian ethics. The general religious movement somewhat loosely designated as "liberalism" or "modernism" has considerably less vitality than it possessed a generation ago but still raises a protest which should not be ignored. The characteristic anti-theological bias, or anti-dogmatic character, of this movement tends to reject a large part of theology as futile hair-splitting. Reacting against the excessive contentiousness which has beset the Church, these advocates of Christian morality and personal devotion would put an end to theological disputation and dogmatic activity.

Caught in the cross fire of criticism from its own camp, denounced on one hand in the name of faith and on the other hand in the name of ethics, theology would find its function reduced to the vanishing point if it were to seek to conform completely to the wishes of its critics. Theology must not abandon its activity because of this challenge. To do so would be to deprive the Christian community of one of its essential safeguards. Whitehead has observed: "The witness of history and of common sense tells us that systematic formulations are potent engines of emphasis, of purification, and of stability. Christianity would long ago have sunk into a noxious superstition apart from the Levantine and European intellectual movement, sustained from the beginning until now. This movement is the effort of Reason to provide an accurate system of theology. Indeed, in the outlying districts where this effort at rationalization died away, the religion has in fact sunk into decrepitude of failure.

"Thus the attack of the liberal clergy and laymen, during the eighteenth and nineteenth centuries, upon systematic theology was entirely misconceived. They were throwing away the chief safeguard against the wild emotions of superstition. . . . History has authority so far, and exactly so far, as it admits to some measure of rational interpretation."[15]

There can be no serious question of the truth of Whitehead's contention that intellectual effort is necessary in preventing the deterioration of religious devotion into superstition. It is also true, however, that a completely philosophized religion can become irrelevant sophistry or barren gnosticism unless it preserves consciousness of the place of reverence, faith, commitment, and action. Consequently, the challenges from within the Christian community should not be brushed aside but heeded. Reduced to rather simple terms this challenge can be presented in the form of three questions: 1. By what method, other than that of unquestioned acceptance of ecclesiatical, traditional, or Scriptural authority, do you propose to determine the true answers to questions regarding man's ultimate nature and destiny? 2. Why do you presume to speculate and explore these theoretical questions when you might well confine your interests to the practical problems of Christian living? 3. How do you propose to reduce to systematic formulation those supernatural truths which are, by definition, superior to the rational constructions you must use to produce your system?

Because these questions are both sincere and plausible, it is incumbent upon theology to justify its activity to the Church.

The Challenge to Theology from the Secular World

Like the protest to theology from within the Church, the challenge to theology from the secular world tends to be an epistemological query: "By what method do you derive the statements which you present to us as true, and in terms of what criteria do you propose that the alleged truth of them may be tested or verified?" This challenge comes from a world which is familiar with several fairly clearly defined procedures of inquiry and with the propositions which have been produced by these procedures. While the religious challenge to theology turns largely upon the work as a *human enterprise,* the secular challenge calls in question the *truth, intelligibility, comprehensiveness,* and *coherence* of the theological accomplishments.

The extent and significance of the secular challenge are

intimately associated with the development of science and of the scientific spirit within the past four centuries. This is not to say that it has been the aim or intent of science to discredit theological inquiry. The result has been the by-product of scientific investigation. Whether intended or not, however, the net effect has been to provide a basis for calling in question the competence of theology.

There are three forms in which scientific advance has raised the question of the validity of theology. First, though not most important, is the fact that scientific inquiry has rendered judgments regarding phenomena and has offered explanations which do not coincide with traditional theological propositions. Second, there is the defining of a method of inquiry which has no definite limits of extensionality and which may be taken as the uniform path of knowledge. Third, perhaps most important, there is the development of several philosophical systems which have taken their inspiration from science and have advanced criteria of judgment which would brand theological propositions as false, inconsequential, or unintelligible by their very nature.

One of the most impressive and distinctive characteristics of the Western world during the past four centuries has been the steadily growing body of factual information—observationally derived and empirically vindicated—which seems to deserve, in every sense of the word, to be designated as genuine "knowledge." The descriptions of the events and forces of nature, together with the generalized expression of uniform behavior which they evince, have been the basis for most of the material progress of modern history. The significance of this for theology is that no small part of these judgments of science have been advanced in direct contradiction of classical theological affirmations. Theology has presented conclusions about the nature of man and of the physical universe, statements made on the strength of religious authority or derived deductively from basic postulates. The fact that science has found a way of drawing conclusions on these same cosmological and anthropological questions and the fact that these scientific judgments have won almost universal acceptance at the expense of the corresponding theological propositions have done much to discredit the whole theological enterprise.[16]

It certainly is not necessary to recount in detail the rearguard action which has been waged in the name of religion against the successive pronouncements of science. It has been a rather sorry picture of defending as final and absolute truth those elements of theological system which pertain to the nature of celestial motion, the age and shape of the world, the continuity of organic being, the nature and cure of disease. The oft-repeated pattern of response on the part of theology in the face of empirical data which goes contrary to theological expectation is first to reject and attempt to suppress the offending information; when that becomes impossible, to construct *ad hoc* explanations to account for the information; and, finally, to announce, "This really wasn't an essential point of doctrine." It is little wonder that after a series of such events a general suspicion should arise that theology lacks any valid method of justifying its affirmations.

Theology can take small comfort from the fact that quite a number of "scientific judgments" have had to be rejected or revised, some of them in the direction of classical theological affirmations. The fact that the scientific presentations never claimed for themselves anything more than tentative certainty affords a flexibility which enables science to revise its conclusions by the same means it reached them, and to do so without loss of prestige. Theology, on the other hand, having claimed to speak in terms of eternal truth cannot escape the indictment of having failed in its endeavor.

As serious as have been these particular issues of fact in the impact of scientific thought upon the reliability of theology, a more significant factor is the defining and extending of the method of scientific inquiry. These past centuries of scientific progress have been characterized not only by the accumulation of definite bits of information but by an increasingly clear definition of method of inquiry and verification, and by an extension of the area in which that method produces reliable judgments. In fact, almost any person identified with scientific activity would insist that science is not to be equated with any particular body of factual information but with the method by which those facts are determined.

As this approach to knowledge has subjected itself to examination and criticism it has recommended itself as a valid means of investigation in ever-widening areas of human interest. Empirical and inductive inquiry has proved its reliability in the area of organic being as well as in the range of mechanics, and it has its strong advocates as *the* way to knowledge in the fields of sociology and psychology. It is frequently contended, often over the objection of the theologian, that the scientific method is valid for matters of ethics and religion. The question naturally arises, Is there any reason for supposing that this does not constitute the one reliable approach for all human questions? If the concrete cosmological judgments of science challenged theology by indicating that some of its conclusions were unreliable, the definition and extension of scientific method poses the more serious question of whether its entire activity is not superfluous.

Theology can ill afford to side-step this challenge by an appeal for "spheres of influence," by an effort to acknowledge the supremacy of science in one field but insist upon its exclusion from others. This frequently takes the form of a disjunction of "matters of fact" from "judgments of value" and of assigning to science the task of investigating all matters of quantitative definition while reserving for theology the realm of the non-physical. D. C. MacIntosh has characterized this attempt: ". . . from the very beginning of modern scientific research there have been those who have tried to secure for the dethroned 'queen of the sciences' a sheltered realm beyond the reach of empirical investigation, within which she might dogmatize to her heart's content—a realm of 'over-beliefs,' concerning which the scientist as such must remain agnostic, but which, it is triumphantly maintained, he is as unable to disprove as the theologian is to prove. Thus many modern scientists are benevolently disposed to patronize theology by handing over to her the undisputed possession of such fields as are supposed to be hopelessly beyond the reach of human experience."[17]

Efforts in the direction of the mutual exclusiveness of science and theology are legion—and uniformly unsatisfactory. The Thomistic designation of the full autonomy of reason and experience in the "natural" realm, and the authoritative reign of dogma in the "supernatural" realm, is an artificial disjunction. The effort of Schleiermacher to confine theology to the level of "religious feeling," and of Ritschl to maintain "religious value" apart from historical or metaphysical fact, both had their motivation in the desire to secure for theology some domain safe from all current and future criticisms or encroachments on the part of science. It is quite possible for an individual to find a degree of security in such a limitation of theology and in confining religion to some sort of aesthetic reference. He may even feel constrained to share Santayana's conclusion that to attempt to ascribe any *literal* truth to religion involves a forfeiture of all symbolic and moral validity. Whatever the individual may choose to do in this respect, the Christian community as a whole cannot accept such a position without denying the genuine relevance for life of the major part of its doctrinal heritage.

When science is recognized either as a body of empirically determined knowledge or as a method of investigation, it calls in question the conclusions and validity of theology. It is, however, certain philosophical systems generally associated with the scientific orientation which most directly challenge the soundness of theological inquiry. Metaphysical and epistemological theories which have taken their lead from natural science have presented serious intellectual problems for all religious thinking. We have in mind materialistic monism, pragmatism, and analytic philosophy. Each of these has been able to borrow a certain amount of prestige from the accomplishments of science itself and to claim a sort of identification with the scientific endeavor.

The theoretical and practical accomplishments in the fields of physics, mechanics, and astronomy in the seventeenth and early eighteenth centuries gave impetus to a wave of dogmatic materialism. Naturalistic philosophies arose which won increased favor as principles of uniformity became apparent in the areas of chemistry, biology, and certain of the social sciences. It is a matter of considerable historical interest to review the effect of these philosophies upon religion and philosophy. The doctrinaire mechanism, strong as it once was, is hardly a matter to be reckoned with at the present time. It would be too much to assert that theology thoroughly refuted its position. More accurately we would recognize that its superficiality was self-defeating. The same scientific movement which once made it seem plausible eventually rendered it untenable. Its significance for theology at the present time lies only in its lasting effect upon the popular mind.

Of far more contemporary importance is that derivation of

British empiricism which has taken root and matured in American philosophy as pragmatism. The significance of its critique is not to be measured so much by the profundity of its system as by the extent to which it has become a pervading, though perhaps unconscious, element in the general thinking of the country. Pragmatism is as frankly materialistic as were the older mechanistic philosophies. It, like them, draws its inspiration from natural science and differs primarily in the fact that it tends to look to biology for its guide rather than to mechanics as did the older forms of naturalism. The "root metaphor" (to borrow a term from Pepper) of materialism was the machine; that of pragmatism is the organism. The organismic interpretation of society and the evolutionary concept of life furnish the model for the structuring of the system.

There are many particular conclusions of Christian theologians and pragmatic philosophers, especially in the area of ethics and societal organization, which have been mutually irreconcilable. Most serious of pragmatism's influences, however, has been its contention that theology's approach is not so much erroneous as futile and pointless. The central critique of pragmatism is that questions concerning *ultimate* aims, values, and truths do not constitute a proper field for human inquiry. The task of human reason is confined to searching for the solution of immediate practical problems; speculation or inquiry into "truths" or "goals" which lie beyond the pressing concerns of social existence is but a misdirecting of energies. Pragmatism is not necessarily antireligious. It accords to religion definite pragmatic or utilitarian importance; a societal function which serves to promote and conserve certain socially recognized values. This reappraisal of the place of religion, according to Dewey, renders superfluous the systematic and theoretical constructions of theology. "It signifies that a religious attitude would sur-render once for all commitment to belief about matters of fact, whether physical, social, or metaphysical. It would leave such matters to inquiries in other fields. Nor would it substitute in their place any fixed belief about values, save the one value of the worth of discovering the possibilities of the actual and striving to realize them."[18]

The challenge of pragmatism is, in a sense, an invitation and a bit of advice. It is an invitation to abandon as futile all preoccupation with the "pseudo-problems" of ultimate aims and values, of metaphysical explanation, and of supernatural concerns in favor of a limited consideration of instrumental values. The underlying proposition is that scientific method-ology constitutes the only approach to real knowledge, that this method should be extended to the investigation and solu-tion of all problems of social and personal character as well as physical, and that in any matter with which science is not pre-pared to deal no questions should be raised. The proposal of pragmatism, then, is that the results of scientific inquiry, how-ever tentative, be accepted as the only form of knowledge which is available to us and that, therefore, any matter not subject to inclusion within the domain of science be acknowl-edged as a "pseudo-problem."

There is enough common-sense appeal in the dictum, "There is no point in raising questions you don't know how to answer," to give to pragmatism a sharp cutting edge against theology. Whatever may be its shortcomings as a compre-hensive philosophy, and they are many, pragmatism has be-come a strong undercurrent of modern thought which tends to put theology on the defensive.

Both mechanistic materialism and pragmatism are over-shadowed as philosophical movements by the contemporary emphases of analytic philosophy. If there can be any one fea-

ture which deserves to be accepted as the distinctive characteristic of modern philosophy, it is the analytical approach.[19] In
the English-speaking world it tends to hold a place of undisputed pre-eminence. Because it has won the support of some
of the most creative and rigorous minds of the twentieth century, analytical philosophy may safely be regarded as a force
to be reckoned with on the present intellectual scene, and one
which may be expected to exert a long-time influence.

For our purposes it is possible to classify under the term
"analytic philosophy" a fairly wide range of philosophical
movements: logical positivism, logical empiricism, semantic
analysis, ordinary-language philosophy, and a number of sub-
groups which have historical or conceptual ties to the so-
called "Vienna Circle."[20] Among these various "schools" there
are significant differences of approach. However, in terms of
the challenge which they present to theology they follow the
same basic pattern.

Analytic philosophy is primarily concerned with the critical
examination of the meaning of various forms of communication and with the specification of modes of verification. It
acknowledges its debt to certain older philosophical movements; the Hegelian system, though subjected to scathing
criticism, is the starting point for much of its technical investigation. The influence of British empiricism is apparent. Although the specific formulations of the Kantian system are
emphatically rejected, the spirit of the first critique is continued, at least in its negative aspect. Hume stands out as the
greatest single point of reference; his reduction of knowledge
to "relations of ideas" and "matters of fact" constitutes a
dictum for the logical empiricists and for most analytic
philosophers.[21]

Even as materialism and pragmatism drew upon mechanics
and biology for schematic interpretation, so analytic philoso-

phy identified itself closely with the field of science, particularly mathematical logic and theoretical physics. Through Mach and Schlick the ties to scientific methodology are strong, and most analytic philosophers have accepted the scientific procedure as a model for correct thinking, at least so far as existential judgments are concerned. In a sense the movement merits the criticism of reducing philosophy to the function of furnishing epistemological footnotes to scientific inquiry.

The dramatic development of mathematical and symbolic logic during the past century has been an essential aspect of the philosophy of science and has been appropriated by the analytic philosophers as furnishing them with the sharpest tool so far placed in the hands of critical thinkers. It has not only resolved certain of the perplexities of the older logic but has made possible the more precise analysis of propositions which proved awkward for classical modes of expression. The significance of this development seems to be only dimly recognized by many theologians. The situation which faces the Church today seems comparable to that which confronted it in the twelfth century upon the reintroduction of the Aristotelian *organon*. At the mid-point of the twelfth century it seemed necessary for the scholar to choose between being a Christian and a logician, and it is not surprising that for a time the Church forbade the study of Aristotle. The turning point in Scholasticism was the appropriation by Albertus and Thomas Aquinas of the logical revolution and the application to theology of the Aristotelian method of synthetic reasoning. The employment of modern symbolic logic by analytic philosophy confronts Christian theology with a challenge similar to that which was produced by the Aristotelian revival and calls upon the Church to recognize the critical tool of propositional analysis.[22]

The dual reliance upon scientific procedure of verification

and the analytic potentials of symbolic logic imparts to analytic philosophy its distinctive character. The limitation of intelligibility and of cognitive meaning to statements which are empirically verifiable, or are in the form of logical tautologies, is but another way of asserting that the only significant, or even genuine, propositions are those which are scientific in character, or are some form of linguistic definition. Although there exist some pronounced differences of opinion concerning the "strength" or "weakness" of the empirical verification which can impart meaning to synthetic propositions, and equally sharp disagreement concerning the intrinsic or arbitrary quality of logical relationships, the insistence upon clear empirical or formal verification is consistent.

There is, of course, no fundamental necessity for accepting the restriction of intelligibility to these two categories, and it is entirely possible to level counter-criticism against the analytic schools as advocating standards which are to a high degree arbitrary. No small part of the traditional interest of philosophy is automatically excluded, and Casserley's observation seems fully justified: "For sheer contemporary dogmatism, commend me to the logical positivists! . . . it seems to me a pseudo-humility when a man irresponsibly resigns a kingdom in order to become the autocrat of a farm."[23] Of equal force is the charge made by Julian Hartt: "Philosophy has fallen upon evil days because of its preoccupation with methodological questions. It seems to have got lost in the endless mazes of epistemology and logic, and to have nothing better to do than to examine with microscopic subtlety the structure of language. . . . The grand result appears to be that the philosophers take in one another's washing; each examines the semantic and linguistic respectability of the others' questions about questions and statements about statements."[24]

Whitworth College Library
Spokane, Washington

The dogmatic restriction of the field of philosophy and the triviality of the results of much that passes for philosophy is the basis for a just criticism of analytic philosophy. The fact still remains, however, that by focusing critical attention upon the problem of determining the meaning of abstract propositions, this movement has raised certain questions which theology cannot afford to ignore.

Metaphysical web-spinning and grandiose system-building after the manner of Hegel have come in for some scathing criticism at the hands of analytic philosophy. On the whole, this has been a highly beneficial influence both in pointing out rhetorical evasions and in making specific the particular quality of meaning which is characteristic of scientific generalizations.[25] In fairness, it must be admitted that theology frequently stands in need of critical review for the sake of exposing those deliberate mystifications and linguistic befuddlements which find their way into religious as well as philosophical writings. The demand that theology confine its utterances to a form of communication which is genuinely intelligible, and indicate the quality of meaning which adheres to them, is not an unfair challenge. It is not unreasonable to ask whether or not theological propositions are proposed as "meaningful" in the sense that they can be subjected to empirical validation, or whether they can claim only the formal validity of logical structure.

Many, perhaps most, representatives of analytic philosophy go beyond the raising of the question, however, and are prone to assert as a strict characterization that theological statements, like those of metaphysical nature, are utterly without cognitive significance, complete nonsense, because they are neither synthetically formed with reference to empirical verification nor analytically reliable as restricted to linguistic definition. A. J. Ayer may be taken as a fair spokesman of this charge.

His position is somewhat less restrictive than that of Schlick or Wittgenstein but is more explicit than that of certain of the advocates of "ordinary-language philosophy."

The basis of Ayer's indictment of theology rests upon his assertion that no statement involving synthetic judgment can have literal or cognitive meaning unless there exists some conceivable method of empirical verification, some sensory evidence which can confirm or refute it.[26] (We may ignore, for the time being, Ayer's consideration of the formal truth-value which rests simply on logical structure and involves no synthetic judgments.) Literal meaning is possible only for a statement which is conceivably subject to some type of sensory confirmation or refutation. Metaphysical assertions, statements about the ultimate nature of reality as it lies beyond the range of sense experience and is inaccessible to empirical examination, cannot be taken seriously as possessing any meaning at all. The linguistic form of expression may bear all the external characteristics of a sensible statement, but it is actually nonsense. "For we shall maintain that no statement which refers to a 'reality' transcending the limits of all sense-experience can possibly have any literal significance; from which it must follow that the labours of those who have striven to describe such a reality have all been devoted to the production of nonsense."[27]

Religious or theological statements, like metaphysical statements, if they offer no empirical reference must come under the same judgment. The possibility of religious knowledge, if this be taken to be of transcendent character, is ruled out. Statements about the existence of God are completely devoid of any cognitive meaning. They are neither true nor false, not even probable.[28] Ordinary sense experience offers no possible means of validating or refuting the statements, and an appeal to some form of non-sensory perception breaks down as soon as an effort is made to communicate that perception. "If one allows that it is impossible to define God in intelligible terms, then one is allowing that it is impossible for a sentence both to be significant and to be about God. If a mystic admits that the object of his vision is something which cannot be described, then he must also admit that he is bound to talk nonsense when he describes it. . . . We do not deny *a priori* that the mystic is able to discover truths by his own special methods. We wait to hear what are the propositions which embody his discoveries, in order to see whether they are verified or confuted by our empirical observations. But the mystic, so far from producing propositions which are empirically verified, is unable to produce any intelligible propositions at all. And therefore we say that his intuition has not revealed to him any facts."[29]

Assertions regarding ethical obligation and eternal life, like those regarding a transcendent God, since they have no possible empirical verification, must be regarded as neither true nor false but devoid of literal meaning.[30] It is quite possible for sentences to have hortatory or emotive significance; in fact, it is just such meaning that our moral utterances do have. For Ayer, the assertion, "stealing is wrong," is nonsense if we suppose that it constitutes a proposition. It can derive meaning only if we understand ourselves to be saying, "Don't steal!" or, "I disapprove of stealing." It is his conviction that "those philosophers who fill their books with assertions that they intuitively 'know' this or that moral or religious 'truth' are merely providing material for the psychoanalyst."[31] Theological statements, therefore, at least in so far as they touch upon any subject which is metaphysical, transcendent, or ethical, are without cognitive significance; and if they are taken to be hortatory or emotive utterances, it is pointless to inquire as to their truth.

If the restrictions on meaning and intelligibility which analytic philosophy demands were to be accepted, it would follow that the function of theology would be virtually eliminated. It is in no sense incumbent upon theology, however, to accept these limitations. The logico-empirical definition of "meaning" is unnecessarily arbitrary and needs to be expanded not simply for the sake of theology but for a large part of significant human thought.

The challenge of analytic philosophy, however, does not arise from its having produced the criteria to which all thinking must conform. Rather, it confronts theology with the demand, if it find the logico-empirical standards inappropriate, that it indicate what criteria of meaning and intelligibility *are* adequate and appropriate. It is an old story for theology to assert that, since it deals with matters which lie beyond the range of reason and experience, it cannot be subjected to the tests of reason and observation. This is not necessarily an evasion. If, however, it protests against the imposition of extraneous criteria, it is called upon to indicate what standards are to be employed in the construction and criticism of its judgments.[32]

The problem that arises when we seek to judge a construction by inappropriate standards is not peculiar to theology. We encounter the same thing in the field of aesthetics if a critic objects to a painting; "This work is not good. There are such things as white horses, brown horses, black horses—horses of many shades and colors—but you have painted horses blue. There are no such creatures." The painter may reply that the critic is seeking to judge by literalistic standards which do not reflect the true aims of artistic expression. His protest carries no weight, however, unless he is able to define in some manner the standards by which the picture *can* be judged. Similarly, the theologian may seek to impose his criteria upon some other discipline. He may say to the mathematician (and the illustration is not fictitious), "Your value for π is wrong. The Bible teaches us that circular objects have a circumference exactly three times the diameter. You should adjust your calculations to conform to revealed truth." If the mathematician rejects this imposition, as he must, then he is called upon to indicate the empirical or geometric standards according to which his work may be criticized and tested. Analytic philosophy cannot insist that its standards of intelligibility and meaning are the only ones, or that it is incumbent upon theology to test itself by those standards. It can and does challenge theology to the task of specifying its criteria of meaning and truth.

Theological Response to the Contemporary Challenge

The contemporary challenge to theology, though significant in its quality and intensity, presents a situation which is neither novel nor unique. That theology be subjected to criticism both from within the Christian community and from the secular world is characteristic of every age in the life of the Church. In the case of the current criticism, as in the past, it is unquestionably true that the response to challenge is best presented in positive rather than negative terms. This means that the strongest reply which theology can offer to its critics comes simply from its continued vital functioning. When members of the Christian community assert that human systematizations cannot deal with divine truth, the best answer lies in a sincere effort to produce formulations which are adequate and coherent. When scientific accomplishments tend to raise the question of the competence of theology to present any form of genuine knowledge, the most effective answer lies in the presentation of information which can commend itself as true. When various schools of philosophy proclaim that theological utterances are devoid of relevance or of meaning or of intelligibility, the most constructive response is that of producing formulations which obviously are relevant, intelligible, and meaningful.

It is neither possible nor desirable for theology to take upon itself the exclusive task of meeting in detail each criticism leveled against it. To do so would be to become hopelessly involved in secondary considerations. It cannot undertake to meet every antagonist on his own terms. To do so would involve making itself a segment of the movements which have challenged it.[33] Most, if not all, of the challenges to theology are met by the simple performance of its historic role.

This does not mean that theology can ignore the fact that it has been subjected to criticism or the form which the criticism assumes. There are dangers involved in excessive concern to answer every specific charge, but there are even greater dangers involved in assuming that all indictments may be brushed aside as presumptuous interference, or ignored as passing fads. If theology is indifferent to the intellectual climate in which it speaks, its productions may be both profound and honest, while it has, at the same time, permitted its work to become hopelessly remote and irrelevant. Although, as is generally recognized, theology is a function of the Christian Church and addresses itself to the community of faith, it cannot remain aloof from contemporary intellectual struggles which take place outside the Church; in doing so it would forfeit its appeal to a large part of the Church as well as lose its ability to speak to the secular world. Although theology neither requires nor expects that all its conclusions shall commend themselves to those who do not share its presuppositions, it must seek at least to be comprehensible to any person who will examine its formulations.

To a degree theology shares in a problem which belongs to the whole intellectual fabric of the times, the breakdown of communication between various branches of human inquiry. Paul Holmer writes: "An argument presupposes two points of view and two arguers. But the irony is that the church's dialogue is actually an instance of the church talking to itself, a monologue as it were. And there is no one to convince because no one is really listening."[34] In a similar vein Casserley observes: "I can think of no danger in the contemporary intellectual situation more alarming than certain perceivable tendencies of a very real Christian intellectualism to become of so inbred and introverted a character that it has nothing to say to the world about anything in which the world is interested, and no interests of its own which anybody else would conceivably entertain."[35] It is to this same concern that Karl Heim addresses himself in his efforts to stimulate a theological awareness of the implications of changes in scientific concepts.

Twenty centuries of history bear witness to the importance to Christianity of being aware of secular challenge and responding to it. Every generation has known some measure of criticism, and over the centuries these attacks have been blunted. This fact, however, offers no basis for complacency on the part of theology. The attacks have been blunted simply because theology took cognizance of them and endeavored to deal with them in some constructive manner. As often as not it profited by appropriating a part of the insight of its critics. It is just such a response which Holmer recommends: " . . . it seems incumbent upon contemporaries to address themselves to the theological fundamentals in a new and radical manner. Certainly the Christian tradition gives ample precedence for precipitating the unpredictable. . . . Christians ought not to tremble before the contemporary breakdown of the intellectual framework, for such an event is not the specter of bankruptcy. The spirit of Christianity gives the strength to practice a certain flexibility and especially in respect to all subordinate matters and to ally one's self with whatever may be best for the understanding and statement of the Christian faith in any moment of time."[36]

Against the background of a sophisticated Greek world patristic Christianity found it impossible to confine itself to confessional statement and was driven to polemic discussion. Only by effecting some reconciliation with Platonic and Stoic concepts was it possible to turn the edge of pagan criticism and to communicate the essential message of Christianity to the Western world.[37] A similar flexibility was manifest in the Scholastic appropriation of Aristotelian science and logic, a successful meeting of an intellectual challenge which has left its mark on Protestant as well as Roman Christianity. Subsequently, the rise of Renaissance humanism with its semi-pagan affections challenged the other-worldliness of existing formulations and offered a competing system of reference. It was only by recognizing the significance of the humanistic movement and appropriating certain of its features that Christianity adjusted itself to the demands of the modern world. More recently the deistic and idealistic philosophies[38] posed threats to Christian convictions, threats which have been met primarily because theology was aware of their criticism and chose to acknowledge their relevance for the formulations of Christian doctrine.

The successive challenges of the past have been met by a response from theology which involves rejection, adaptation, and appropriation. There have been certain features of critical movements which had to be met head-on, which called for direct refutation at the hands of the theologian. Other criticisms had to be acknowledged as justified and as calling for genuine revision on the part of theological statement. This has called for discernment on the part of the Church, for a discrimination between those criticisms which are leveled against actual weaknesses in the theological structure and those which are simply the product of blind prejudice. It also demands on the part of the Church a confidence in the essential soundness of doctrine which can submit itself to re-examination and criticism without fear of its destruction.

It should be clearly apparent that the theologian cannot submit either to the pragmatic suggestion that theology abandon all concern with ultimate questions or to the analytic dictum that it acknowledge all transcendental affirmations to be nonsense. There is no possibility or genuine necessity for conceding that the inductive-empirical method of natural science constitutes the only valid method of inquiry in any area of knowledge. All such dogmatic restrictions call for direct refutation. This is a part of the methodological task of theology.

It is not enough merely to protest against the imposition of inappropriate criteria or to point out the weaknesses of those formulations which challenge theology. It is important to specify as clearly as possible just what constitutes theology's means of construction and verification. If there is to be any distinction between "good" theology and "bad," between "false" and "true," there must be some criteria which are acknowledged as competent to confirm or refute theological affirmations. "Adequate methodology is a basic need of both modern research and creative thinking. Method cannot give us a new spirit, but it can free the spirit from confusion and false burdens."[39]

Unless Christian theology is to be content with fighting rear-guard actions against scientific developments and with defending one outpost after another (always contending that the last engagement really was not a decisive one), it must be prepared to make explicit the basis on which its affirmations are presented. Unless it is willing to withdraw into some area of irrelevant speculation, it must define the criteria by which its pronouncements are to be judged. Unless it is content to let contemporary philosophy speak one language and theology another, with the consequent loss of all possibility of communication between the two, it must examine and explain the quality of meaning it claims for its propositions.

The challenge which comes to theology both from the Church and from the secular world raises the twofold question of what matters theology proposes to consider and the justification it is willing to claim in those areas where it makes pronouncements. Does theology have any peculiar area of concern and raise questions which it suggests constitute the exclusive domain of its discipline? Does it propose to make pronouncements about matters which are subject to empirical investigation? If we can define the area in which theology operates, we must deal with the more difficult problem of the description of the method which is appropriate to its inquiry. Does theology claim some distinctive methodology, determined by its field of interest, which enables it to draw and substantiate its conclusions; or does theology simply employ the methods which are used by other disciplines and subject itself to the same criteria?

If there is something about the approach of theology which makes it distinctive and which imparts to its propositions meanings peculiar to it, then it is important that such features be made plain. If there are certain problems peculiar to theology which make it impossible to judge its findings by the ordinary standards of truth, then the proper standards need to be specified. Ordinarily we assume that the method by which truths are derived can serve as the method by which they are to be tested. If the standards of rationality or empirical observation will not serve, then it is imperative to indicate what criteria will serve.

If, on the other hand, theology simply employs the same methods of inquiry which are accepted and employed in other fields, that fact should be made clear. If theological propositions are derived and commended as rational propositions, they are subject to the criticism of logical rules. If they are derived as empirical facts, then they can be submitted to observational refutation or confirmation.

In an "age of analysis" the crucial task of theology is to undertake on its own behalf an analytic work. So long as the basic approach is called in question there is little profit to be found in simply extending the number or variety of conclusions which are drawn. Traditional affirmations which have been challenged by having their means of derivation discredited or confused cannot be buttressed simply by a rephrasing and extending of them. If the conclusions of theology are to carry weight in a century in which method is a matter of major concern, then it must be by some clear awareness of the characteristics, potentialities, and limitations of the approach which it employs. Its concern must be to show as specifically as possible the nature of the inquiry it proposes to undertake, the scope of its interest, the method by which it endeavors to reach conclusions, and the extent to which it is willing that the same method which is used for derivation shall be used to criticize its findings.

Theology is not to be understood as one limited branch of inquiry which makes in its restricted field some contribution to the sum of human knowledge. Rather, it is the effort to incorporate and relate all forms of knowledge, natural and revealed, with the view to giving some intelligible answer to the question of the ultimate meaning of life.

In this comprehensive sense theology cannot demand that science and philosophy provide those specific conclusions which will serve the purposes of theology. It can, however, integrate the objective judgments of science and philosophy within the context of human response and decision.

THE SCOPE OF THEOLOGY

THE justification of theology as a serious human enterprise and the vindication of its claim to present truths
which are both intelligible and relevant demand a clear
exposition of its scope and method. In the face of the contemporary challenge, if it is to meet without evasion the
attack of its critics, theology must undertake to state un-
equivocally both the nature of its inquiry and the procedure
which it deems appropriate for that inquiry. This means that
it endeavors to answer directly the dual question: On what
subject, or subjects, do you propose to speak, and what is
your basis of competence to speak in this area of interest? To
whatever degree theology is able to give a satisfactory answer
to this question it may expect to command the serious consideration and respect of the modern world.

The question of the *scope* of theological concern is, in a
sense, prior to that of *method*. The two are, of course, interwoven, but a clear definition of the range of interest will
serve to determine or point to the method appropriate to that
field. If we can specify the form and range of the problems or
questions to be investigated, we have taken a major step in the
direction of defining the procedure which can be expected to
produce reliable information or understanding.

There are presumably two ways in which theology can

point to the scope or nature of its task. One way is to make clear to itself and to its critics the particular goal to which it aspires. The other is to define the specific questions it endeavors to answer. Its methodology, then, will consist in the conscious adopting of the procedure which is designed to attain that goal or give answers to the questions which it has seen fit to raise. It is needful, therefore, both for the exercise of its function and for the sake of communication with other fields, for theology to re-examine and redefine in terms of the present generation its objectives and its scope of interest.

The Aims of Theology

Theology, as a systematic expression of Christian faith and knowledge, has throughout the history of the Church rather clearly recognized both constructive and polemic goals. It must, so long as faith seeks understanding, provide the Church with constructional formulations through which the Church apprehends and communicates its message. To this extent it speaks for and to the Church. However, it must also be able to speak for the Church to the secular world, and this means that it must always acknowledge an apologetic aim. The challenges to the message of the Church are conceptual in nature and call for a conceptual response. This is not a matter of contentiousness but is a realistic awareness of the fact that these challenges must be responded to if the Church is to endure.

Kenneth Foreman states this twofold aim most effectively:

"We take up our parable from the story of a practical man, Governor Nehemiah. His workmen were all provided with two implements, a sword and a trowel. They had to be equally ready to build and to fight. So today the theologian . . . must have his sword and trowel. Theology must be both polemic and constructive. Theology which is only polemic goes around chopping off heads; its aim may be accurate and its thrust deadly, but it builds no abiding city. Theology armed only with the trowel may be driven from the scene by some invasion of alien ideas, and so leave the city in defenseless confusion. . . .

"Now just as in Nehemiah's day the builders worked with sword on thigh, so today theology has to work with sword as well as trowel. The sword does not build the wall; nevertheless no sword, no wall. So long as there are enemies about, wanting some other kind of wall, or no wall at all, we shall have to keep the sword by us. . . .

"The work began before any one of us was born. We shall all rest from our labors in due time, but the work will never rest. We cannot see around the long circuit of the walls; but we know that the workmen are there, and we can be grateful."[1]

The constructive aim of theology is essentially one of supplying an adequate vehicle of *communication,* of producing a formulation which makes possible the transmission of knowledge, insight, or understanding. It is not, therefore, to be regarded as the production of information or insight but as the production of an adequate medium of expression. To this end theology seeks formulations which are intelligible and coherent, not as if formulation were a goal in itself but because structure, clarity, and coherence are essential to communication. In this construction it must aspire both to be faithful to that insight or understanding which belongs to the Church and to the ordinary conventions which make communication between human beings possible.

The apologetic aim of theology, like the constructive, is basically one of communication.[2] It must speak to the secular world in defense of the message of the Church, and it must speak in a fashion which can be understood and appreciated by the critic. This places theology under an additional restriction when it is functioning apologetically. It must, in speaking to the secular world, confine itself to those concepts and conventions which the world is ready to accept. Its aim is to accommodate itself to those criteria and standards which are recognized as the common and valid references of truth. It was in this spirit that Origen adopted the language of Hellenistic philosophy for the sake of conversing with the world in which he lived and that Augustine, though protesting that it involved "beginning at the wrong end," was willing to restrict himself in his apologetic writings to the thought-forms of the pagan world.

It is only fair to concede at this point that the two aims of construction and apologetic are not always accomplished by theology. There exists the basis of protest that the formulations of theology have not been sufficient to incorporate the whole of the Christian witness. In the same manner it must be recognized that the apologetic function is never entirely successful; not every critic is either silenced or converted. We are speaking of *aim,* and even where this is not attained, the goal must be acknowledged. Theology must aspire to be as convincing as possible, but even where the limitation of speaking within the restrictions of the critic makes it impossible to be fully *convincing,* it must at least assume the task of making itself *intelligible.*

To the constructive and apologetic aims of theology we must add a third, the critical aim. The function of criticism is not completely distinct from the other two; it tends, rather, to be subordinate or instrumental with reference to the others. Even in this instrumental frame, however, it looms large at this time by virtue of the criticisms which are characteristic of this century.

In pointing to the critical aim of theology we may press Foreman's parable a bit further and suggest that the effective use of the trowel calls for someone to hold a plumb line. If it is to be able to distinguish "good" theology from "bad," it must have at its disposal some critical apparatus which it knows how to employ. It would seem necessary for theology to develop and indicate the standard of reference which may be of most value. Unless it is prepared to accept externally imposed standards, the theologian must be prepared to designate his "plumb line" and to conform to it in every respect. This is nothing more than the self-regulative restriction which is essential to any discipline.

Karl Barth has designated this critical function as the essential characteristic of "dogmatics." Its task is that of examining the language with which the Church speaks about God.[3] *Dogma* is one form in which the Church speaks, and *dogmatics* consists in the subjecting of that expression to the tests of communicative adequacy as well as to the essential standard, faithfulness to the Word of God.[4] In this sense, for Barth, theology functions as a critical "science" and recognizes as its primary task that of defining and applying the critical apparatus in terms of which the proclamation of the Church is to be judged, corrected, revised.

One need not argue that Barth has placed too narrow a limit upon the work of theology in excluding the constructive function from "dogmatics." The Church must *present* the message which dogmatics undertakes to criticize, and the formation of the mode in which it is presented may be designated as something other than "theology" if one chooses. It seems, however, that the functioning of theology is best described if one is willing to recognize the constructive and apologetic goals, as well as the critical aim. Theology speaks for the Church as well as to it.

The Comprehensive Field of Theology

We may define the scope of theology by reference to its constructive, apologetic, and critical goals as they relate to the proclamation of the Church. We come to a sharper definition if we are willing to undertake a description of the subject matter with which theology proposes to deal. Here we approach directly the question, What questions do you raise and in what area do you inquire and make pronouncements?

Any detailed answer to this question which aspires to be accurate as well as precise must be prefaced by the assertion that theology is literally concerned with *everything*. There is no subject of human concern which is by its nature or the nature of theology excluded from consideration. To say this is to do more than assert the obvious truth of the interrelatedness of knowledge. It is to claim for theology a genuine comprehensiveness of interest which is its most distinguishing mark. This is not to propose that theology possesses a special key to knowledge, applicable in every field, which is available to it alone. It is rather to acknowledge that there is no type of knowledge significant and relevant for men which is insignificant or irrelevant for theology; that therefore theology is, in a real sense, *dependent* upon all forms of inquiry.

It is in recognition of this comprehensiveness of theology that Paul Tillich writes concerning the manner in which the "preliminary" concerns of science and philosophy become the bearers or vehicles of the "ultimate" concern of theology. "That which is a finite concern is not elevated to infinite significance, nor is it put beside the infinite, but in and through it the infinite becomes real. *Nothing is excluded from this function.* In and through every preliminary concern the ultimate concern can actualize itself. *Whenever this happens, the preliminary concern becomes a possible object of theol-*

ogy. But theology deals with it only in so far as it is a medium, a vehicle, pointing beyond itself."[5]

There is something of the same indication of scope in Barth's assertion: "All the sciences at their acme might be theology."[6] To whatever degree human inquiry follows its path in the direction of examining, explaining, expressing "language about God" it has become a part of the theological activity. Only as this objective is ignored or kept in the background out of practical considerations can any form of knowledge be said to exist separate from theology.

If we try to regard theology as genuinely restrictive, as is sometimes done etymologically by insisting that its scope is limited to "knowledge about God," the artificiality becomes quickly apparent. Our considerations must involve not only God *in se* but God in all His relationships as Creator, Preserver, Redeemer. Immediately we are involved in anthropology, ethics, history, cosmology. These considerations are not incidental but constituent to theology.

This comprehensive character of theology is borne out if we undertake to describe it by reference to the subjects treated by theologians; to indicate the scope of theology by saying, as it were, "It's what theologians write books about." The Apostle Paul wrote about "church-night suppers" and women's hair styles. Bishop Berkeley wrote lengthy discussions of the medicinal merits of tar water, Kierkegaard concerning the art of courtship, and Pascal upon the betting-odds at horse races. This is not intended as a caricature. The theologian *as a person* may have interests as broad as the whole range of human curiosity, and there is no way of specifying which of these interests could be excluded from the designation "theology." Every theology is, potentially at least, a *summa*. The limits are accidental rather than intrinsic in the sense that they are determined by the knowledge and interests of the person rather than imposed by anything essential in theology.

While there are certain subjects which are commonly recognized as being of special interest to theology, there are others, seemingly remote, which under certain circumstances come within its immediate province. The study of falling bodies, the examination of the nervous system, the composition of music, are ordinarily considered to lie within the realm of physics, medicine, or art. However, if the "falling body" be a bomb, if the examination of the nervous system involves subjecting individuals to experiments which may be destructive of personality, if the composition of a piece of music involves the awareness of response to various types of music, then these matters are of importance to theology. It is not enough to assert that the lines of demarcation are vague; the indefiniteness is due to the fact that no such lines exist.

The Distinctive Field of Theology

If we assert this comprehensiveness of theological interest, is it denying that there exist any particular concerns which impart a distinctiveness to the discipline? To say that it is concerned with *everything*—is not this another way of admitting that it is concerned with *nothing* in particular? Are there no fields of primary or exclusive jurisdiction in which theology claims a special competence to speak?

We must reaffirm at the outset that *it is this very comprehensiveness which is the most distinctive mark of theology.* If we first make this point clear, it is then possible to designate certain areas of interest which are characteristic of theology as a distinct discipline.

There are several significant contemporary approaches to furnishing a description of this specifying feature of theology.

Paul Tillich settles upon the designation of "ultimate concern" as the essential feature of theology. By this he means that theology is working in its special and distinctive province when it is inquiring into the final and irreducible problem of "being as over against not being." While he emphasizes that knowledge from any and all fields may be brought to bear upon this one ultimate question, he recognizes that there is a need for theology to heed the common sense advice for the "cobbler to stick to his last." The theologian has his hands full if he undertakes seriously to examine and express this problem of "ultimate concern"; he may find it a practical necessity to leave to others the examination of those matters of instrumental importance and be willing simply to appropriate that part of their work which he finds immediately relevant for his own special problem.

"The object of theology is what concerns us ultimately. Only those propositions are theological which deal with their object in so far as it can become a matter of ultimate concern for us.

"The negative meaning of this proposition is obvious. Theology should never leave the situation of ultimate concern and try to play a role within the arena of preliminary concerns. Theology cannot and should not give judgments about the aesthetic value of an artistic creation, about the scientific value of a physical theory or a historical conjecture, about the best method of medical healing or social reconstruction, about the solution of political or international conflicts."[7]

Karl Barth finds the distinctiveness of theology in the fact that it takes as its field the examination of the language of the Church about God. He rejects the notion that theology can be made one science among others in the sense that it is a branch of some broader line of inquiry, but considers that it does have a field of special concern with respect to the Church's proclamation. If we can recognize that the Church's proclamation in its turn has as its primary function a statement about the act and manifestation of God, then we can say that this same area is the prescribed field of theology.[8] The *kerygma* is not made up of all the utterances which have come from the Church but is the central message about God's creative and redemptive act. It is this upon which the inquiry of dogmatics focuses, and all other considerations become significant for theology only as they tend to throw light upon this central consideration.

In both Tillich and Barth the distinctiveness of theology rests upon the end to which it incorporates consideration of the wide range of human interests. Whether we regard it as "interpretation of the *kerygma*" or "concern for the ultimate," we are viewing the specific scope of theology as an interest in that which is of final interest, that which cannot be understood as a means toward some other or broader knowledge. In these two cases it could hardly be said that there is a pointing to areas of inquiry *separate* from the other concerns of men; rather to that inquiry which is the *correlation* and *integration* of all forms of investigation.

There are two suggestions of definite areas of inquiry, somehow inaccessible to other disciplines, which indicate a peculiar domain of theology. One way of indicating this special consideration is that employed by J. V. L. Casserley in declaring that theology undertakes to treat seriously "the problem of the singular." This means that theology can deal with that which is unique, preserving its uniqueness by refraining from an attempt to make it an example of some general classification. Philosophy and science are prepared to deal with "particulars" and "universals," but they cannot deal with a reality which is genuinely unique. Theology, however, because of its identification with an historical faith (and the historical focuses attention upon those very unique features which escape science and philosophy), must give attention to singularity as well as to particularity and universality. An extended quotation from Casserley focuses attention upon the effort on the part of theology to deal with the "singular" as an object of knowledge:

"The advent of Christianity forced a new problem upon the attention of the ancient world—the problem of the singular. Greek thought had ignored this problem, or rather, had looked it in the face and then turned its back upon it, dismissing the singular as something which was incapable of becoming the object of knowledge. Thus for Plato, or perhaps more accurately for the Platonic Socrates, individual entities were the object not of scientific knowledge but of mere drifting 'opinion.' Aristotle is more realistic in the frank recognition that the individual entity is the unit of perception and existence, but even for him the individual is unknowable as such. 'Perception must be of a particular, whereas scientific knowledge involves the recognition of the commensurate universal.' The very habit of describing the individual as the 'particular' is significant of the ineradicable bias of the Greek mind toward the universal. Thus for Aristotle, in spite of his 'realism'—using the word in its modern sense—the individual is only knowable, can only be thought, in so far as it can be regarded as a particular instance of a universal rule. There is a profound distinction between the term 'particular' and the term 'singular.' The particular is the individual as seen by the man who is looking for the universal, and who will feel baffled intellectually until he finds it; the 'singular,' on the other hand, is the individual seen from the point of view of the man who is out to capture and enjoy the full flavour of its individuality. In other words, and using the word rather broadly, the particular is the individual seen through the eye of the empirical scientist, whereas the singular is the individual seen from the historian's point of view; but not the historian's only, for the bias toward the individual is one which he shares with the dramatic writer, the metaphysician, the theologian, the religious devotee, and the ordinary man in his everyday concern about his fellows.

"This general overlooking of the problem of the singular, so characteristic of Greek thought, had an important effect upon Greek logic, which has influenced the teaching of logic to this day. . . . Because it failed to take proper note of the problem of the singular, Greek logic recognized only two kinds of proposition, from the point of view of quantity, the universal and the particular."[9]

Although Casserley makes his point through a contrast of Christian and classical Greek thought, the same basic distinction serves to indicate a peculiar domain of theology. The *uniqueness* of theology lies in its serious endeavor to deal with that which is *unique*. Two illustrations will serve as examples of this feature of theology: it deals with the Incarnation not as a particular instance of a general class of incarnations but as a unique event; with the Trinity not as a special instance of mathematical relationships, or even of interpersonal relationships, but *sui generis*.[10]

Casserley is, of course, correct in emphasizing that the serious consideration of the "singular" is not confined to theology alone; that the historian and the artist are particularly conscious of this mode of being. What is peculiar to the theologian, in contraposition to the artist and historian as well as to the scientist and philosopher, is that he treats this mode of being as the object of genuine knowledge.

Nels Ferré employs other terms in indicating the distinctiveness of religious thinking. (Although the terms "religion" and "theology" are not synonymous, there is no violence done in this instance by the transposition of words.) The field of theology, though at many points overlapping and including other areas of interests, reaches out on its own to accord special significance to what may be designated as "whole-response" or "commitment of self."[11] Here, of course, we are touching on the traditional theological emphasis upon "faith" as a form of knowing. However, at this point we are not examining *method* so much as *scope*. Ferré would have us see that theology determines to call in question the general, and often obscured, supposition which underlies all non-theological inquiry—the assumption that all true knowledge is somehow to be identified with objectivity. In so doing it claims for itself a realm of inquiry which treats "response" of subject as an integral part of that which is known.

One need not challenge the propriety of proceeding in areas other than theological upon the assumption that objectivity is essential to understanding. Complete detachment, absence of the bias imposed by preference and subjective inclination, quite properly belongs to the more restricted fields of human inquiry. Even though it be recognized that complete objectivity is unattainable, it remains an important aspiration of empirical and rationalistic examination that it be reduced to the least possible point. Theology does not fulfill its function by seeking to exclude this responsive element but by undertaking to make it a significant element in its considerations. For this reason the current emphasis upon the "existential" quality of theology does not represent a fad but points to an essential aspect of theology.

Existentialists may err at times in seeking to exclude from Christian exposition everything except the subjective and non-systematic, in making rational order into a natural foe of religious truth. They are right, however, in calling attention to the fact that theology, unlike other disciplines, has made the whole-response of the individual a significant ingredient of truth. To describe the existential element as "essential" to theology is to use the word in its classical sense; the *essence* being that which imparts uniqueness or self-identity to any form of being. To regard this quality as essential to theology is no more an exclusion from it of all objective knowledge than the designation of man as a *rational* being is a denial of his physical body or of the fact that he shares with animals the capacities for motion, reproduction, and the assimilation of food.

To describe, then, the scope of theology is to indicate that it undertakes to deal with the ultimate question of being. To this end it must, of necessity, draw within its range of concern all knowledge of any sort in so far as it bears relevance to such final determination. Its own distinctive contribution must be made in that area which is ordinarily excluded by other disciplines, the field of personal commitment; for this, too, must enter into its consideration of the ultimate. The scope of theology includes the *appropriation* of that knowledge which is available from all other inquiries, the *contribution* of its special insights in the realm of the response of self-commitment, and the *integration* of the whole as it bears upon the final question of existence.

The Relationship of Science, Philosophy, and Theology

Even though, for the sake of distinctiveness, we may attempt to specify the area in which theology functions with reference to a primary interest, it is necessary to return to the initial affirmation that its specificity lies in its very comprehensiveness. To say that it is concerned with the final or ultimate question is to recognize that it must interest itself in all contributory knowledge. To say that it has a particular interest in the whole-response of personal commitment is not to restrict itself to a particular type of subjective experience, but rather to say that it has recognized this as relevant for its total task. Theology does not simply seek to add its peculiar contribution to the sum of human understanding but rather undertakes to acknowledge and appropriate all forms of knowledge, its own contribution among others, for the sake of an integrated understanding of the ultimate meaning of life.

Only in such terms of inclusiveness is it possible to designate the scope of theological interest and activity. In these terms, too, it becomes possible to indicate the relationship which exists between theology and those other aspects of human inquiry, science and philosophy. To claim for theology this comprehensive interest is to assert that the work of science and philosophy is not something *other than* theological inquiry but something which is *contributory to* and *continuous with* the theological enterprise.

This, of course, is no more than a reaffirmation of the "medieval synthesis." The ancient ordering of levels of inquiry placed theology in a position of pre-eminence which made all other disciplines subordinate to its concerns. The fact that this synthesis has broken down in the Western world does not mean that the basic concept was false. Many factors, not the least of which was theology's own misinterpretation of what was involved in this "subordination," contributed to the breakdown of this structure. A false autocracy produced a false autonomy. The false assumption that theology's inclusive concern made it competent to prescribe the conclusions which might properly be reached in less comprehensive fields produced a situation in which it was necessary to disassociate scientific and philosophical inquiry from theological restrictions. No one would deny that this disassociation has made possible independent advances on the part of science and philosophy which could not have been possible so long as theology was able to impose restraint upon their enterprise. But this has also resulted in a disintegration and confusion; a disintegration in the strict sense of loss of coherence and unity, confusion in the sense that immediate goals have been pursued without awareness or consideration of any ultimate goals or meaning.

Science has for its scope all those aspects of our experience which are *empirical* in their reference and *immediate* in their presentational form. It has developed and specified a methodology appropriate to the field of its inquiry. This empirical, immediate character of its subject matter may further be described in terms of the public, objective, and quantitative features of its data. Its domain is restricted to that which can have some sensory reference, which can be expressed in mathematical formulation, and can be checked by anyone who is willing to undertake the project. The limitation of field is recognized and accepted for the sake of deriving a particular kind of knowledge. When these limits are overstepped, science has moved outside the field of its competence. We should be quite careful, however, in determining in advance that some particular matter cannot be brought within the scope of scientific inquiry. In blunt language, science is quite competent to investigate any matter in which it can find sensory qualities which it can measure. Efforts to delimit science from all considerations of human personality, society, ethics, or even religion considered as a social phenomenon, have proved futile—and quite properly so. Each of these areas contains pertinent data which is subject to empirical investigation.

The scope of philosophy is broader than that of science and inclusive of it. The medieval designation of what we now generally speak of as "science" under the title of "natural philosophy" serves to indicate the inherent relationship of the two disciplines. Philosophy, properly understood, includes all scientific investigation and presupposes that the conclusions of science are to be incorporated within its formulations. The "understanding" which is the goal of philosophy transcends the "knowledge" of science not in the sense that it scorns it or condescends to it but in the sense that it undertakes to incorporate this knowledge in a broader context of meaning. In its outreach beyond that which has been made the subject of direct empirical verification philosophy must draw into its orbit the consideration of that which is logically possible as well as that which is observationally confirmed. It must employ speculative inquiry into the inferences of empirical knowledge and venture propositions about the nature of things as they lie beyond any recognized means of direct verification.[12]

Even as science may undertake to investigate any matter which furnishes empirical data, so philosophy may properly undertake to speak on any matters which are subject to rational formulation and the criticism of logical relationships. For philosophy, as for science, we should be cautious in making advance judgments which would designate fields in which it is incompetent to deal. In any area in which philosophy may find it possible to discern logical relationships and to formulate a rational system of explanation it may quite properly function. This means that the concepts of religion, to whatever degree they are presented as rationally formulated constructions, may be brought within the critical scrutiny of philosophy as to their clarity and consistency.

The field of science includes all that part of experience

which is *immediate* in nature and *empirical* in reference. Even where the term "science" is employed to describe that which borders on the metaphysical, the dealing with abstract formulations which are not themselves immediately perceived, there must be some empirical base for the constructions and some theoretically possible means of verification by reference to immediate sense data.[13] Philosophy must reach both back into the field of science and beyond it into the area of speculative construction. It reaches back into the field of science not in the sense that it proposes to conduct independently all the investigations of science but in the sense that it examines, criticizes, and explains the method by which science operates. It reaches beyond the scope of science in the sense that it seeks to determine certain logical inferences beyond immediate empirical investigation.

Both science and philosophy must strive to preserve objectivity and detachment in the course of their inquiry. Although complete objectivity is unattainable, the validity of scientific and philosophical work is proportional to the elimination or discounting of personal preference and subjective bias. This means that a definite limitation of scope is accepted. "What I want to be true" contributes nothing to my investigation; on the contrary, it may well stand in the way of my reaching reliable conclusions. There is no escaping the fact that preferential judgments are involved to some degree in almost all human thinking, but science and philosophy must endeavor to ignore or exclude these judgments from their considerations.

In the same manner that philosophy includes or transcends science, it is in turn transcended by theology. Theology incorporates not only the empirical conclusions of science and the rational formulations of philosophy but also those existential or subjective considerations which the others perforce ignore. It asks not only the immediate questions of science and the penultimate questions of philosophy but also the ultimate question of the meaning of human existence. In contradistinction to science and philosophy it not only may, but must, take into consideration the response of personal commitment to some final end and the preferential judgments which are neither empirically based nor logically derived, but nevertheless underlie the immediate and penultimate determinations. The more reflective scientist is led to raise cosmological and epistemological questions which are of philosophical nature, and the more curious philosopher will always keep reaching out toward the ultimate. "Just as every man in so far as he speculatively interprets the world is a philosopher, so every man in so far as he is ever aware of the thoughts of his whole-thinking is a theologian . . ."[14]

We need to keep in mind that when a person moves outside that area in which he can tie his constructions to concrete empirical data, he is no longer functioning as a scientist; when he seeks to explore into final problems which are not reducible to objective rational formulation, he is no longer functioning as a philosopher. The converse, however, is not true. The philosopher, as a philosopher, may quite properly raise and examine questions which lie within the range of empirical verification. Similarly, the theologian has not forsaken his role when he engages in empirical and rational investigation. So long as he keeps in mind the relevance of the finite for the infinite, so long as he does not permit preliminary considerations to obscure the ultimate consideration, so long as he does not make the mistake of according to the preliminary considerations a final status, the theologian has a proper concern for the factual knowledge of science and the rational understanding of the philosopher. The relationship of scope of science, philosophy, and theology in terms of successive inclusion may be indicated:

SCIENCE	PHILOSOPHY	THEOLOGY
Empirical	*Empirical and rational*	*Empirical, rational, and existential*
Immediate	*Immediate and penultimate*	*Immediate, penultimate, and ultimate*

If for the sake of common sense we need to recognize that theology is not called upon to consider separately every question that can be raised in any field, we do not thereby exclude any field as such from its concern. It is called upon to consider any and all questions *as they may have bearing upon the ultimate consideration.* This means that theology must attempt to discover what, if any, significant import any question, scientific or philosophical, has for ultimate determinations and to deal with it in that light. Unless the solution of a chess problem should contribute in some way to an understanding and exposition of man's final destiny, and it is difficult for me to construct a hypothetical situation in which this would be true, the theologian certainly isn't called upon to consider it. There are within the field of science and philosophy no end of problems which are "outside" the range of theology in this same sense, practically excluded because the relevance is so remote as to make their consideration pointless.

Dangers Arising from a Comprehensive Definition of Theology

The scope of theology can be indicated only in inclusive terms. To do this, however, presents certain dangers, the possibility of misinterpretation of what is meant by this comprehensive undertaking. The first of these misinterpretations has already been mentioned as an historical occurrence, the medieval assumption that the "higher" discipline is privileged to dictate the procedure and conclusions of the "lower" inquiries. Theology is always beset by the temptation to look upon itself as occupying a particular vantage point from which it can discern just what scientific or philosophical insights will contribute best to its own formulations and accordingly to insist upon those specific conclusions. Like a Procrustes it demands that science and philosophy trim or stretch themselves to fit a theological bed.

There is a certain plausibility to the assumption that the more comprehensive interest is determinative of the subordinate ones. Ever since Plato there has been a bias in the direction of regarding Truth as somehow proportional to generality. Accordingly there is the tendency to view with suspicion or categorically deny those particular conclusions which do not support the generalized formulation.

Whenever theology has presumed that its more comprehensive concern makes possible a prior determination of the proper conclusions of science and philosophy, its influence has been in the direction of producing a complete separation of concern and accomplishment. The disintegration of Western culture into diverse patterns of thought which have lost the capacity for intercommunication is due in no small degree to the effort to impose "from the top" the appropriate findings of the subordinate fields. The revitalization of the physical sciences in the fifteenth and sixteenth centuries could not produce its fruit so long as the sciences were expected to produce the particular conclusions which fitted the dominant theological framework. At a later date the biological sciences found "open-ended" research incompatible with the requirement to conform to a prevailing religious orientation. Similarly the social sciences, psychology in particular, encountered the difficulty of keeping in communication with a theology which wanted a certain kind of findings.

The blunt historical fact would seem to be that any serious endeavor on the part of theology to prescribe the appropriate conclusions of science or philosophy has resulted in some form of "break." The independence necessary for empirical inquiry resulted in a separation of interest and termination of communication. For theology to speak *imperialistically* has been but an invitation to a general questioning of the propriety of theology to speak *at all* on such matters.

We understand the true comprehensiveness of theology only as we reject this notion that inclusive interest carries with it the privilege of dictating subordinate conclusions. Instead of being in a position to prescribe findings for the more comprehensive interest, it is *dependent* upon the subordinate disciplines. The theologian has no access to empirical facts which are hidden from others. In dealing with physical phenomena he has no basis of judgment except that of scientific inquiry; he may either accept and use the findings of the scientist or endeavor to determine them for himself *by exactly the same procedure employed by the scientist.* What theology has to contribute to this knowledge is unique only in the sense that it can draw into consideration factors which are not themselves scientific.

There is nothing within the objective criteria of science which can justify judgments concerning the penultimate and ultimate ramifications of its inquiry. From the scientific point of view there can be no negative judgment concerning the propriety of subjecting a group of human individuals to torture for the sake of determining their level of resistance. The detonation of a thermo-nuclear bomb in an inhabited area for the sake of learning the effectiveness of the weapon has a "scientific" reliability as an experiment which is determined only by the care and precision of the observations which are made. The subjecting of a "control group" of children to emotional strain for the sake of determining its effect on personality development has a scientific justification which is determined only by the reliability of the measurements involved. These "scientific" matters do come within the scope of theology—*not, however, in the sense that theology has a different and better way of learning the effects of physical or emotional strain.* When theology asserts an interest and an *authority* in the scientific realm, it does so in terms of taking into consideration broader ramifications than can be brought within the confines of science, not in the sense that it can claim a superior wisdom as to what the facts are. It can call in question the propriety of certain scientific experiments, not because they are scientifically unsound but because they are theologically inappropriate.

For theology to claim, by virtue of its inclusiveness, even this sort of *authority* is not to claim *infallibility*. It is worth while to recall that there have been theological pronouncements, often backed by ecclesiastical and civil power, against the "violation" of the human body either for therapeutic surgery or physiological research. There have been theological protests against the use of narcotics. There have been theological pronouncements against scientific "invasions" with reference to the reliability of religious documents or to the interpretation of historical and archaeological evidence. The fact that these protests have been sincere does not alter the fact that they have been falsely restrictive. The recognition of its fallibility should not lead theology to abandon its function of comprehensive criticism, but should be a motivation for the exercise of humility and caution in an area where it has often been in error.

Not infrequently theology has taken upon itself the right

to define the conclusions which philosophy as well as science may derive. Properly sensing that there is a relationship between the penultimate judgments of philosophy and theological judgments, it has sought to have philosophy supply a particular set of propositions which logically imply the conclusions of theology. Actually, this approach is a reflection of one of the most common of logical confusions, that of seeking to affirm an antecedent on the strength of an affirmed consequent. Theology recognizes that certain philosophical propositions, ontological and epistemological, would imply those propositions which theology affirms. Asserting the truth of its own propositions, it seeks to affirm on that basis the truth of those propositions antecedent to them. This form of intellectual imperialism is as tragic in its effect as it is logically fallacious. It serves only to create a situation in which philosophy must disassociate itself from theological inquiry.

This first misunderstanding of the manner in which theology comprehends science and philosophy is the presumption that it occupies a vantage point from which it can anticipate the proper conclusions of the subordinate disciplines. The second misunderstanding is closely associated with the first. It is a tendency on the part of theology to *identify* itself with some particular scientific or philosophical formulation.[15] When theology takes seriously the fact that its interests include those of science and philosophy, it is a simple matter for it to assume that it must "include" some specific scientific or philosophical body of material. It undertakes with a degree of success the task of establishing valid relationships between its doctrines and the empirical and rational theories of a particular school or stage of inquiry, identifies itself with the vehicle which it has found convenient, and then is extremely reluctant to consider the possibility of any other vehicle. This, as is almost universally recognized, took place with reference to Hebrew moral philosophy, Platonic metaphysics and Stoic ethics, Aristotelian biology, Ptolemaic cosmology, and, more recently, idealistic metaphysics. As a side comment it is also possible to observe that there is a corresponding tendency for theology to identify itself at various periods with particular political, economic, and psychological schools.

The way in which this misunderstanding may be avoided is through a stress upon the fact that the comprehensiveness of theology involves the inclusion of the process of inquiry of the subordinate disciplines rather than an inclusion of those specific theories or formulations which have a temporary prestige. Theology cannot afford to ignore what seem to be the strongest empirical and rational constructions at any given time. It must accord to them essentially the same respect which is claimed for them by the discipline through which they have been produced. It is foolish, however, for theology to *bind itself* to these conclusions when neither science nor philosophy has presented them as anything more than tentative hypotheses or plausible generalizations. For theology to employ contemporary scientific and philosophical insights as the best available media of its formulation and communication is one thing. For it to accord to such insights its uncritical and unyielding allegiance is quite another thing. This latter course presents the strange picture of theology's claiming the right to pass judgment upon the conclusions of science and philosophy and in the exercise of that function placing itself under the dominance of the very disciplines it has undertaken to regulate.

The assertion that theology comprehends these other disciplines is not to conclude that it offers some special way of determining the truth of empirical judgments or of rational constructions. Neither does theology incorporate into itself any particular body of scientific explanations or philosophic constructions. Rather it is a recognition of the fact that theology must take full cognizance of these fields of endeavor, not as separate from its own concern, but as contributory to the most intelligible formulation and presentation of the meaning and end of existence.

The Practical External Limit to the Scope of Theology

If, as is contended, theology is restricted from no field of inquiry except as it chooses to leave apart those considerations whose relevance for ultimate determinations is obviously remote, there still arises the possibility of an external limit of scope in the sense that there is an area which lies even beyond theology. Are there not reaches of truth which transcend its concern even as theology transcends science and philosophy?

So long as we are willing to preserve our designation of theology as an inquiry into *truths which are of ultimate concern to men* (see page 24) the assertion of its *ultimate* character would preclude the possibility of there being something beyond it. If, however, we take seriously the designation of theology as a *human* enterprise which aspires to *intelligible* and *coherent* formulation, we must recognize that these serve as qualifying and limiting terms.

The very fact that the work of theology is a task undertaken by men seems sufficient to assure that its scope is limited to what men can grasp and communicate. We need not stress that this be a "grasp" in terms of any special capacity of man, experiential, rational, or mystical. It is impossible to conclude, however, that a human enterprise has the possibility of incorporating that which lies beyond human prehension. The finitude of the men by whom and for whom theology is undertaken places a limit beyond which it can have no aspiration or endeavor.

More to the point, however, are the limits of intelligibility and coherence. We are not called upon to insist upon any highly restrictive meaning for this "intelligibility." There is no requirement that theology present its results in such a form that its conclusions are inescapable. As DeWolf observes, "Christian theology, well expounded, should be reasonably *intelligible* to an educated and diligent student who is not a Christian. But many of its evidences are not likely to seem *convincing* to him unless some Christian who witnesses to their truth has become for him an authority in such matters."[16] The distinction is important. Certainly theology cannot limit itself to that which all men will recognize and accept as true, but it can draw within its enterprise only that which it is able to communicate in some intelligible form. It might seem unnecessary even to mention this point except for the fact that there appear to be individuals bent upon providing men with an understanding of that which no man can understand.

If we add to this the further designation of theology that it involves *coherent* formulation, we are faced with an even more limiting requirement. We are saying in effect that the scope of theology is confined to that which can be brought into some structured unity. Again, we may refrain from imposing a rigid description of this coherence, whether complete logical consistency and mutual entailment of all propositions is called for or not. There exists at least the requirement that theology shall present more than a disordered array of unrelated propositions and *non sequiturs*. Theology is limited to that which it can *relate* in the same manner that it is limited to that which it can *make intelligible*.

This is a special problem for theology because it has ventured to draw subjective commitments into its considerations. Existentialists, Christian and non-Christian, have been right in their insistence that certain truths of existence become distorted by any effort to reduce them to systematic formulation or force them into rational or substantial categories. Their ridicule of the philosophic presumption to overcome all antinomies and to resolve all uniqueness into broad generalities is merited; and even more justifiable is the protest against the assumption that theology can force all divine activity and purpose into the categories of a rationalized structure. Clearly there are aspects of the Christian faith which escape the most extensive and subtle of theological formulations. To reduce them to a coherent pattern is to change them. Existentialism, however, can exceed its warrant if it makes inconsistency a criterion of truth or excludes systematic formulation from the proper realm of human inquiry and discourse. To make absurdity the prime ingredient of Christian truth is hardly the way to accord honor to God or significance to the human response to His demands.

Theology may freely acknowledge that its systematic expressions have never been able to capture, contain, or elucidate the so-called "mysteries of faith." It may with equal frankness confess that it possesses no scheme whereby it proposes to reduce all transcendent truth to the confines of human understanding. This is not to acknowledge *a prioristic* limits or to specify particular matters with which theology is not competent to deal. It is rather to say that even as science may properly claim an area of investigation anywhere that it may find anything that it can measure, theology may extend its scope to all that it can formulate coherently.

The logical "proof" presented in 1932 by K. Gödel that no logical system can be both comprehensive and consistent seems to have satisfied all subsequent logicians. The coherence which theology endeavors to supply stands, in a way, at cross-purposes with the comprehensiveness to which it aspires. In this situation theology can establish its claim only to that truth which it can coherently express even while acknowledging the possibility of a reality which escapes its formulations. All forms of factual knowledge, all rational constructions, all aspects of the subjective commitments of self as they can be coherently related to an understanding and intelligible presentation of man's ultimate concern, lie within the province of theology.

From Scope to Method

The definition of scope and the description of method are, as was indicated at the beginning of this chapter, inseparable. The extent of competence of theology is best described not by a listing of subjects to be examined or by pointing to a set of propositions but by indicating a method of inquiry. The scope then will be coterminous with material which can be brought into that form of investigation. Even as science is a method of procedure rather than a body of facts, and philosophy a manner of construction and criticism rather than a particular system or sum of systems, so theology is to be identified with a method of deriving, vindicating, and integrating those truths which can contribute to an understanding of the final meaning and goal of life. The defining of that method is the central feature of what has already been designated as the *critical* function of theology. (See p. 62.) Either theology must simply accept that its approach, together with appropriate criteria, is the same as that employed by science or philosophy or must make explicit its own method. It is hardly possible that the method of theology is identical with that of any other discipline; if that were true, theology would then be simply one aspect of the designated discipline rather than a comprehensive inquiry. If, on the other hand, it has a distinctive method which can be defined and for which appropriate criteria can be specified, then it is in a position to regulate its own activity in terms of criticism and construction and to give an answer to those critics who challenge its competence.

On the basis of what has been said about the comprehensive nature of theology it would seem that there are several specific questions which need to be answered relative to theology's method. In dealing with empirical data and logical constructions, in the field of objective knowledge and understanding which it shares with science and philosophy, does theology have some distinctive way of knowing, or is its method identical with that of the included disciplines? In dealing with that component of reality which has been referred to as "subjective commitment," in a realm for which it has a concern that transcends that of the objective disciplines, what method can it propose for deriving and vindicating true affirmations? In effecting some coherent and intelligible formulation which relates immediate and penultimate considerations to the determination of ultimate fact and meaning, what is theology's method of integration; more specifically, can it derive this ultimate meaning from contributory knowledge or does it have some special way of determining this final truth and of relating subordinate matters to it?

One further question is involved which, perhaps, is contained in the others: How does theology communicate this formulation? This is contained in the other questions if we take it for granted that the formulation of a coherent structure necessarily involves the presentation of it for consideration. It is a separate question if we conclude that theology employs some special or private form of knowledge which is not inherently available to men. In this case we would be presented with the problem of finding a way of communicating an insight which is not shared by all.

Because of its comprehensive scope, theology must include within its approach those methods which are characteristic of more restricted lines of investigation. Rational analysis, empirical induction, and appeal to objective authority may be seen as having a place in the work of theology. In addition, theology must take seriously a form of subjective certitude which recognizes individual response and commitment as an important element in knowing.

The integration which theology aspires to effect cannot be produced through exclusive reliance upon any one of the methods which has been applicable to some more restricted field. Even though it must be accomplished at the expense of some genuine loss of precision, the convergent judgment of theology is a practical and common-sense synthesis of the results of a variety of methods of inquiry.

THE METHOD OF THEOLOGY

THEOLOGY is a human activity which undertakes to make statements which are *true* regarding the ultimate meaning of human existence. Upon its purpose to present *truthful* formulations turn all the important criticisms of its function and serious challenges to its competence. If theology is to have a place among the serious activities of men, it is upon this claim that it must stand or fall.

Every effort to obscure this goal, or to substitute other criteria for it, is an avoiding of the central issue. An appeal to inspirational value, social worth, antiquity, or aesthetic charm may have some place in reinforcing the claims of theology but not in providing essential justification. It is possible to praise theological utterances for subtlety, profundity, or literary excellence, but apart from their truth value they do not call for serious consideration. Ritschl's effort to disjoin valuational significance from factual truth, and Schleiermacher's endeavor to derive religious statements from emotional reference alone, constitute evasions of the central issue. To follow the advice of Dewey or Santayana that religion reject all involvement with literal meaning or factual truth would be to abandon for theology all claim to genuine significance. One way of pointing this up is in the recognition of the fact that only if theology takes the demand for *truth* seriously can it label any utterances in its field as *false*. Any idea which is interesting can claim equally with any other a place in theology. There can be no such thing as "correct" teaching, no orthodoxy, and certainly no rejection of "false teaching," unless theology is frankly endeavoring to state *truth*.

Accordingly, the method of theology is the procedure for determining and communicating truth. If theology can specify the means by which its statements are derived, together with the criteria appropriate for the criticism of those statements, it has thereby defined the sense in which they are to be regarded as "true." In so doing it provides its own internal controls, the means by which it distinguishes between true and false theological concepts, and the ground on which it is willing to meet the criticisms leveled against it. If its method is one with that of empirical or rational investigation, then it is "meeting the critics on their own ground" in the sense that it accepts the same criteria of judgment. If, on the other hand, it has its own distinctive procedure, then by explicitly defining that procedure theology can specify the standards to which it may be expected to conform. This is to reaffirm the earlier observation (pages 63 ff.) that the exercise of its critical function is essential to the performance of its constructive and apologetic tasks.

Knowledge, Truth, and Certitude

"Knowledge" and "truth" are among the basic terms of discourse. They constitute primitive elements of discourse by reference to which other concepts are defined. Accordingly, it is not to be supposed that either of them submits to entirely satisfactory formal definition. Certainly it is impossible to define either of them without reference to the concept involved in the other. There is a degree of circularity involved in any effort to discuss the two meanings, a circularity which it is not possible to avoid. In the interest of convenience or of some particular emphasis we may take either of them as the primary and undefined term by which the other is specified—just as the mathematician may define a point in terms of the intersection of lines or a line as the locus of a point. There is always some degree of arbitrariness in the choice. Thus when Bertrand Russell selects "truth" rather than "knowledge" as the basic term, he is exercising a proper linguistic right and is doing so with the express purpose of giving a broader meaning to truth than empirical verifiability: "I conclude that 'truth' is the fundamental concept, and that 'knowledge' must be defined in terms of 'truth,' not vice versa. This entails the consequence that a proposition may be true although we can see no way of obtaining evidence either for it or against it. It involves also a partial abandonment of the complete metaphysical agnosticism which is favoured by the logical positivists."[1]

With equal propriety "knowledge" may be made the fundamental term, so long as it is not limited to one particular aspect of knowledge, and "truth" may be employed as a relationship between "knowledge" and a third term, "reality." In the ordinary employment of either term, or in the interrelating of the two, there is involved a necessary illusion, a sort of convenient and conventional fiction. It is the presupposition, already mentioned in connection with the characteristics of science and philosophy, of a complete "objectivity"; a Cartesian disjunction of mental and physical substance in terms of which "truth" or "knowledge" inheres in a one-to-one correspondence between the two. This involves hypostasizing "knowledge" apart from "knower," and "truth" apart from the experience of apprehending. There is no denying that this fiction of objectivity is highly fruitful for epistemological analysis so long as its fictional nature is kept in mind. However, if it be forgotten that there is an ill-disguised contradiction in the very term "objective knowledge," as if it were something subsisting apart from object or knower, then the "truth" which it aspires toward is reduced to an unjustifiable abstraction.

Into the examination of the meaning of the "truth" which theology claims for its formulations it is necessary to inject a third concept, that of "certitude." The connotation of this word openly introduces the element which is frequently denied or ignored when "truth" and "knowledge" are discussed, the element of personal response or reaction. Certitude is the state of confident assurance on the part of a person with respect to some experience, rational construction, or decision. Instead of breaking down the subject-object relationship as is the case when we seek abstract definition of "truth" or "knowledge," when we examine certitude we are concerned with that response to reality which is the basic element of discourse.[2]

Because it is descriptive of a frequently experienced personal reaction, "certitude," unlike "knowledge" or "truth," permits rather simple definition. We recognize it as the state of mind in which we have accepted on some basis (at the moment we need not specify the basis) an assertion and can conceive of no further evidence, of the same or a different order, which would tend to strengthen or weaken that acceptance. I am certain of an immediate experience: other experiences may call in question the *interpretation* I have first placed upon it or may duplicate certain elements of it but can neither confirm nor deny the experience itself. In these terms we distinguish between "knowledge" and "opinion"; opinion may be strongly held, but so long as we "keep the door open" for confirmation or refutation it falls short of genuine certitude, consequently falls short of "knowledge." Similarly, we hold something to be "true" which elicits from us this same unqualified assent which requires no further confirmation and can anticipate no possible basis for revision or refutation.

Theology is concerned with knowledge and with truth. It is, however, knowledge *by someone* and *about something;* truth *for someone* and *about something.* This acknowledgment of subjective reference, knowledge *by* and truth *for* someone, is not claiming for theology any particular exemption from responsibility for the objective reference of knowledge and truth. Rather, it is the recognition that subjective response is involved to some degree in all judgments; that, as Kant made plain, there are both objective reference and mental construction in all judgments, and that neither component can be eliminated completely from any expression of synthetic knowledge. The special relevance of this, however, for theology lies in the fact that, having recognized the subjective as an important element in its area of concern, it cannot subscribe even for practical considerations to the "objective fiction."

The separation of the ontological and the epistemological question, which is fundamental to the "bifurcation of nature" against which Whitehead has protested, expresses itself in our persistent pattern of taking knowledge and reality to be subjects of independent consideration. If, however, it be possible to employ "certitude" or some such term of bi-polar reference as a primitive term, both knowledge and reality may be discussed through reference to this more elemental concept. Certitude, as a psychological state, is directly prehended. Whereas the *awareness of physical reality* is more properly always awareness of *one's impressions of reality,* the awareness of one's psychological state is a matter of direct awareness. In this sense it may qualify as a primitive or undefined term. By reference to it the more complex terms "knowledge" and "truth" can be discussed.

Forms of Certitude

Since certitude of any form involves subjective reference, it is impossible to define exactly what conditions will produce it. There is the "variable" of personal difference which always enters as a significant factor. However, since there is objective reference as well as subjective and since there are certain fairly general features of human response which are somewhat uniform, it is possible to recognize within measure the requirements for certitude.

Two forms of evidence and two forms of corresponding certitude are acknowledged components of constructive and critical thought. These are sometimes designated (1) logical necessity and (2) presentational immediacy. The discernment of logical relationships such that complete coherence persists throughout produces for us a sense of conviction. Similarly, sensory apprehension produces its own corresponding certitude. There is a third form of certitude, less easily defined, which underlies the other two and which is involved in all judgments. It also serves as the ground for practical decisions in those situations where empirical and rational evidence are either non-existent or inconclusive. This is the certitude of unqualified self-commitment.

There is no reason why the familiar term "faith" is not a satisfactory designation of this form of certitude except for the fact that its employment as a religious "virtue" tends to obscure the part it plays in judgments of a wide variety of forms. The volitional or preferential element is clearly present in this form of certitude. Although, as in all meaningful constructions, objective reference is involved, the subjective reference is dominant.

Each of these forms of certitude has its own appropriateness, and no one of them can be completely reduced to the others. In our discourse we are not always explicit as to which of these criteria is being made the point of reference, and not infrequently we seek to reinforce a statement which we regard as important by simultaneously drawing from at least two forms of certitude. Consequently, there often exists some genuine uncertainty about what is intended when we say, "I know this to be true." The affirmations "I know the relationship of the circumference and the radius of a circle," and "I know that the sun is shining," and "I know that my Redeemer liveth" employ similar linguistic constructions but involve distinctly different modes of assurance. There is, however, a common element—that of a certitude, an awareness that there is no evidence of any order which could possibly serve to strengthen or weaken the conviction.

Frequently in nontechnical settings we will say "I know" when we are referring to a state of consciousness distinctly below the level of certitude; and this loose employment may be within the context of any one of the modes of reference. We may say of a rational judgment that we are sure of it when we would be more accurate if we were to assert, "This seems plausible on the basis of a hasty analysis." We may say of an empirical judgment that we know what we've seen when a more correct statement would be, "This is the inference I draw from some rather indistinct impressions." We may say, in an appeal to a certitude which is of the order of self-commitment, that we are sure of something when a more correct statement would be, "I am toying with this as a possibility but not fully committing myself to it." In each case, however, there is the possibility of raising this sub-certitude to the level of logical necessity, empirical verification, or unqualified commitment.

The certitude of *logical necessity* is present wherever strict identity or complete mutual entailment can be demonstrated.

This is the "necessary truth" of Leibnitz, the "*a priori* analytic*" of Kant, the "tautology" of contemporary philosophical analysis. It forms the essential reference for all "geometric" thought, for all deductive reasoning. This form of certitude is always *relational*; it is appropriate for the validation of *relationships* between concepts rather than for individual assertions. No isolated statement or simple proposition is in itself either "true" or "false" in terms of logical categories. Consequently it is always set within a system which relies upon internal coherence, upon non-contradiction, as a touchstone; and it is the system itself which must stand the test of consistency. The essential place which this form of certitude has for the human mind is witnessed to by the persistent effort on the part of philosophers to construct systems which rely upon this as the only criterion and by the universal negative judgment on "inconsistency."[3] The certitude of logical necessity holds a major place in common-sense thought and is not the province of the professional logician alone. In its positive form it impels certitude *if there is no counter-certitude of a different order*. Negatively, it challenges any formally constructed statements. If we ever suggest, "Of course, this is inconsistent, but it is still correct," we are either talking nonsense or are placed on the defensive to show some other criterion in terms of which it may be judged "correct."

The certitude of *presentational immediacy* is the foundation of all empirical investigation and is the point of reference for the bulk of our judgments regarding reality. No matter how much philosophic subtlety may be directed toward the rational vindication or criticism of this form of certitude, its essential impression is neither strengthened nor weakened. It constitutes a "given" which is its own self-authentication. It furnishes the basis for inductive generalization. Special problems arise for epistemology and physiology in connection with those impressions which we designate as distortions or illusions, but the fact remains that the immediate impression of the senses constitutes an essential reference for certitude. I may simultaneously see the striking of a metal disk and hear a tone such as I have been accustomed to hearing from a violin. I may have difficulty in explaining their relationship, but of both the visual and the auditory sensation I am certain.

The inductive inferences from sensory data constitute a form of knowledge which, in spite of our accustomed practical reliance upon it, is not of the same order of certitude as that which is immediately presented. Neither is of the same order as that of logical necessity. The generalized inferences from immediately presented data are properly designated as hypotheses rather than certainties because they present only *possible* explanations of the experiences. Even when prediction is made on the basis of the inferences and those predictions are confirmed, the generalization itself is not transmuted into an "established fact." The efforts of Carnap, Reichenbach, and others to derive a kind of second-degree certainty by an exact calculation of the limits of probability (so that we may be *certain* of the *degree of probability*) do not eliminate the characteristic tentativeness of inductive inference.

For purposes of analysis it is entirely proper to posit both logical and presentational certitude as pure examples of cognitive process. There are, of course, examples of symbolically represented logical relationships and of uninterpreted sense awareness which are of this order. Most thinking, however, involves judgments which go beyond such pure cognitive reaction. Logical certitude extends only to the point of either (1) certifying to the truth of some conclusion *once*

a logically prior condition has been chosen or granted or (2)
indicating conditions which may *not* be jointly held as true.[4]
In practical judgments we must *choose* either the initial
premise which is to serve as a starting point or *choose* from
among the possible conclusions left open by the negative
restrictions of logic. Similarly, in making use of the inferences from presentational certitude we cannot escape *deciding*
what degree of probability we are willing to accept as con-
stituting an adequate basis for judgment or action.[5] Whenever we move beyond the barest skeleton of logic or of
perceptual awareness and undertake to form significant
judgments, we are forced to introduce some degree of subjective determination. There can be no question that there
is a value in reducing this subjective or volitional element
as a factor in judgments. It is impossible, however, to form
anything more than the most elemental constructions without
recourse to some choice.

The Certitude of Unqualified Self-commitment in Theology

Central to the method of theology is a frank designation of
and direct reference to the certitude of unqualified self-
commitment. In part at least, the distinctiveness of theology
lies in this reference—not as sole reference but as significant
reference. Whereas the inevitable injection of subjective
reference constitutes a "scandal" for philosophy and science,
reluctantly acknowledged, it represents for theology an
essential aspect of ultimate determination.

The whole question of the meaningfulness, relevance, and
reliability of theology turns upon the answer to the inquiry,
"In what sense and in compliance with what criteria are these
affirmations to be taken as *true*?" The question as stated must

be rejected rather than answered by theology. It must be rejected because of the awareness that the "objective truth," something that exists apart from subjective determinations, is a false abstraction. It may be a *useful* abstraction within the context of limited inquiry but cannot be preserved in judgments of practical or ultimate nature. In order to answer the question it must be rephrased: "In what sense may I, or any other person, be certain of these affirmations?" So phrased the question can and must be answered by theology. Its formulations incorporate certain references to certitude which is volitional or self-committing in character, and these references need to be explicitly recognized for what they are.

If it were possible to escape from certain of the emotional and conceptual overtones which have become associated with the word "faith," there would be no objection to designating this reference to a certitude of unqualified self-commitment as an "appeal to faith." There are several factors, however, which would seem to make it advisable deliberately to avoid this particular term. Unfortunately there is a tendency to hypostatize "faith" (just as we do "knowledge" and "truth") and assume that it is some sort of objective reality which can serve as a criterion. Further, there is the familiar association of the word with religious attitude exclusively. The additional bias in the minds of some who would equate faith with uncritical credulity justifies caution in employing this term in a description of the method of theology. There is a core of truth in the familiar designation of faith as that which precedes or supplements knowledge, or in the insistence that it constitutes a genuine "way of knowing." We escape from the impossible task of sharp discrimination between "faith," "knowledge," and "understanding" if we deal with the general objective-subjective response of *certitude* and recognize that the *certitude of commitment* is ingredient in all significant judgments.

This form of certitude is the reference of truth or meaning which finds its expression in terms of total responsiveness rather than in a limited cognitive process. We are, in thought process and in unconscious inclination, grasping a form of certainty when we are prepared to act, without reservation or exception, in accord with some concept or principle. This is the kind of "knowledge" which Hans Vaihinger finds unimpeached either by Humean skepticism or by Kantian critique —the disposition and determination to act *as if* certain logically possible and empirically plausible postulations are *so*. Pascal appeals to it as a calculated, but none the less volitional, choice from among various possibilities, a choice which serves as a basis for action. Rall refers to a "moral certainty" which "does not compel us logically or overwhelm us by force; it is rather a challenge to us."[6] Santayana turns to such a psychological certitude as "some irrational persuasion or prompting of life" which is the final arbiter of meaning and our only escape from complete skepticism.[7]

At the risk of belaboring the obvious it is perhaps important to stress that although theology makes a frank appeal to this sort of certitude, it is thereby turning to no criterion alien to non-theological thought process. "Operationalism" in the scientific field is a proposal to employ this same standard. It underlies all naive discourse which makes statements about the future. It is the justification for the methodological assumptions of any discipline. The so-called "objective criteria" set the frame within which certain choices may be made, but they do not eliminate a frank or obscured reliance upon some subjectively defined decision to accept one set of possibilities instead of another as furnishing the basis for action.

The appeal to a certitude of commitment has a special relevance for theology, both in its constructive role of forming judgments regarding the ultimate meaning of life and in its apologetic role of exhibiting and defending those concepts in the face of criticism. In endeavoring to communicate certain insights or concepts of ultimate import, theology is forced to employ as an essential point of reference the commitment on the part of certain human beings to act in a manner consistent with a particular conviction. In defining the sort of meaning that adheres to utterances regarding that which transcends sensory experience it must refer to certain lines of action which belong to the realm of experience. Statements regarding the existence and nature of a transcendent God or concerning a future and unexperienced state of being beyond death are meaningful, and *cognitively* meaningful, in terms of the intent and determination of human beings to act in some particular manner.[8]

The heart of theology's reply to the challenge of analytic philosophy lies in the "meaningfulness" which is imparted to statements by this reference to a certitude of commitment. The restriction of cognitive significance to those statements which are logical tautologies, or which are subject to empirical verification, is an arbitrary insistence upon "playing chess on a board whose squares are smaller than the feet of the pieces; the rules of the game cannot be applied in such case because it remains indeterminate on which square a piece stands."[9] Theology concerns itself with propositions which do have empirical reference, statements about historical events, sensory phenomena, inductive inferences; but it considers these only because they have a bearing upon conclusions which are not empirically verifiable. The conclusions instead of being verifiable are frankly *possibilities,* statements which one recognizes as not subject to sensory confirmation but which are subject to validation in terms of a commitment of self to their implications.[10]

The danger inherent in this appeal to psychological certitude, a threat to which theology has frequently fallen victim, is that it be made the unregulated determinant of judgments. Is anything which I presume or wish to be true thereby certified? Is a commitment to act adequate basis for affirming those realities which would be consistent with the commitment? Taken at face value, an affirmative answer would be to elevate arbitrary choice to the place of final authority.

The safeguard against this danger lies in the fact that theology can constructively deal only with *genuine* choices, determinations which are concerned with real alternatives. Both reason and experience seem to place restrictions as to existing possibilities. Experience precludes the possibility of my living in the first Christian century; I cannot *choose* it. Similarly, logic excludes from my range of choice a commitment of myself to the belief that God is deeply concerned with me and totally indifferent to me.[11] Taken negatively, the criteria of logic and experience serve to define and limit the range of choice, but they do not exhaust the reference of meaning. However, since logical and empirical restrictions still leave open a number of undetermined possibilities, the voluntary acceptance of one or another of these possibilities furnishes the basis for determining lines of conduct and constitutes a reference for meaning and certitude.

Method as Certifying Procedure

Method for theology, as for any other human inquiry, is the accepted procedure for arriving at certitude. If we make explicit the manner in which we propose to derive conclusions and indicate the appropriate criteria which are to be applied, we describe the sense in which the affirmations are to be taken as true or false. To take a rather extreme example: if we decide that lines of action are to be specified by the flip of a coin, so long as we follow a uniform procedure we are applying a "method" of inquiry. There is no guarantee that because it is a satisfactory method for one person, i.e., produces certitude, that it will recommend itself to another person as an adequate form of inquiry. The adequacy of no method can be tested by that same method. (For instance, one cannot determine the "soundness" of coin-flipping by flipping a coin.) This is rather an example of prior volitional determination which underlies all methodology. In specifying the method of theology we cannot thereby assure that it is to produce certitude for anyone; we can only describe procedure and in doing so indicate the context of certitude.

There are three aspects of the method of theological determination. The first is the question of its procedure for arriving at certitude in the areas where its concerns overlap those of other disciplines, specifically in those immediate and penultimate determinations which are of interest to science and philosophy. The second is the manner of reaching judgments regarding those subjective commitments which science and philosophy must seek to ignore, but which theology must seek to incorporate as having significant bearing upon its final determinations. The third is the method of integration: the procedure which can be followed in relating the empirical and rational conclusions, together with the distinctive existential conclusions, to some form of certitude regarding ultimate meaning.

Authority in the Method of Theology

The appeal to some authoritative norm, the reliance in some manner upon a standard which is not itself subject to criticism or correction, is inevitable for any religious formulation which commends itself for acceptance as anything more than a human construction or discovery. Even where theology is recognized as a "human inquiry," it is still seen to rely upon truths which are presumed to be non-human in their origin. So characteristic is the authoritarian element in religious formulations that theology has often been identified with the transmitting of a knowledge which has been divinely imparted. The designation of theology as "divine science" has been interpreted to mean that it is in a position to assert the divine sanction of its formulations as well as the divine character of its object. Certainly there is no major religious community which does not appeal at some point to some form of objective authority as a means of authenticating its affirmations.[12]

The appeal to authority as a "way of knowing" is, of course, not confined to the realm of religion. Reliance upon custom, tradition, general acceptance, or the pronouncements of some person of prestige as affording a reliable standard of reference, is a feature of common judgments. In sophisticated as well as in primitive societies it is an appeal which, though sometimes ludicrous, obviously produces a form of certitude. It is not entirely foreign even to the more rigorous inquiries of science and philosophy. The scientist does not hesitate to cite the observations and constructions of other reliable and respected investigators for the purpose of substantiating his own work. The philosopher turns to the conclusions of the great systems of the past and uses them as a starting point for his own rational investigation.

It would be too easy, however, and entirely unjustified for us to assert: "Everybody has to rely upon the opinions of the expert, and consequently theology is free to designate its 'experts' and accord them uncritical acceptance." We need to keep in mind that although the fact is frequently obscured or forgotten, the appeal to the expert on the part of common sense, science, or philosophy is not strictly a "way of knowing" but a *substitute for* or *short cut to* knowledge.[13] In ordinary, non-technical judgments we are accustomed to rely upon certain sources of information, but always with the reservation that they are subject to refutation or correction if we should decide that it were worth the trouble to apply other tests.[14] This is not genuine *authority*. The scientist, in the interest of time, may feel that it is expedient to accept and employ the observations of others but does not presume that they are subject to no revision or confirmation. The star charts of Brahe may be useful to the astronomer, but he does not hesitate to correct those "errors" which he attributes to the inaccuracies of old instruments. Similarly, the philosopher may "borrow prestige" by citing the opinions of Plato or Kant or may refer to the constructions of classical thought in the interest of pointing to the persistence of some particular idea, but this does not mean that the respected expert has presented a final and normative formulation.

To what extent does theology appeal to an authority which is *not* subject to any critical revision and which constitutes a genuine "way of knowing"? This question poses the problem of whether theology can presume to have access to some superior way of reaching certitude regarding empirical facts or the rational relationship between them, an authoritative reference which is competent to determine for itself what the facts are or imply. For theology to make such an assumption is to pick the quickest and surest path toward discrediting itself as a reliable method of inquiry. The application of authoritative criteria in the determination of facts which are subject to empirical examination is to do nothing more than to project *two* criteria of judgment for the same event, a procedure designed to produce not certitude but confusion. Confusion is exactly the state which has arisen whenever theology has attempted to make an authoritative appeal regarding the facts of sensory experience. When it has assumed that it was in possession either of an authoritative statement of what these facts are or of general truths from which they can be deduced, theology has invited an unnecessary choice between two incommensurable standards of certitude. It is not surprising that it has usually come out the loser with reference to the choice.

The appeal to authority in the area of empirical and rational determination, other than the authority of experience and reason as such, has no place in theological method. As stated earlier, it can claim no special means of arriving at logical or presentational certitude. It is not in possession of any unique sensory data or peculiar insight into logical relationships. This does not mean that theology should heed the advice to leave aside all concern with facts of experience, but rather that it recognizes that its only access to those facts is by means of the empirical investigation open to all men. There is no valid appeal to authority which can contribute to or detract from the certitude of presentational immediacy.

Although we may categorically deny the applicability of an authoritarian method in the determination of experiential facts or logical relationships, we are faced with a more difficult question with reference to the distinctive area of theological concern: the response of unqualified commitment of the individual in which the certitude is inseparably linked to the act of commitment. At this point theology has seemed quite willing to impose one or another authoritative norm. Simply, it has ventured to define the "correct" commitment. Interestingly enough, theologians are in far closer agreement in describing such a commitment than they are in designating the authority which certifies it as *correct*.

When on an authoritarian basis theology ventures to define

a proper subjective response, it does not encounter the difficulty which faces it in injecting such criteria on logic and experience. In this realm there is no confusion of different orders of certitude. Rather, there is the internal difficulty of specifying the authority. There is no need to examine the multitude of ways in which various individuals have sought to vindicate ecclesiastical pronouncements, the canonical Scriptures, or "the inner light" as the formulation of this authority. In each approach there is the willingness to point to one human response, particular or general, as not only typical but normative.

The problem is not to be resolved by an examination of the relative justification for making one expression rather than another the definitive standard.[15] (To subject an authority to external criteria is to surrender the contention that it is an authority.) The only resolution lies in the recognition that "objective authority," like "objective knowledge," is a convenient but fictitious abstraction. "Authoritative," "authority," and "authentic" are relational terms. "Authority" is not a *thing* but a relationship with objective and subjective reference. The tendency to objectify it has been the source of no small part of theological confusion. An authority exists only in the sense that it is an authority *for someone*.

Taken in this sense, it is possible to assert that a designation of authority and conformity to it is made a part of theological determination of the "correct" subjective response of individuals. The theologian can point to the response of commitment on the part of certain individuals and to the corresponding certitude associated with that commitment. He can pronounce this response to be normative in the sense that it represents the condition which is necessary to that certitude. He can indicate that it is *authoritative for the Church* and *for* the theologian who has made the same commitment. Whether or not it is authoritative *for* a particular individual rests entirely with the response of that individual. To speak of "authority" as distinct from such subjective reference is to employ a fruitless abstraction.

Most of what has been said about the application of authority in the area of personal response carries over into a consideration of the place of authority in the determination of the comprehensive problem of theology, the integrating of all knowledge, understanding, and response with reference to that which is of ultimate significance for men. Reason and experience leave open several possibilities regarding ultimate meaning (one of which, of course, is the possibility that there is no ultimate meaning). In endeavoring to define the certitude which we may find with reference to this, theology employs the concept of *revelation*. Its judgment regarding ultimate meaning is presented not as a discovery, a result of methodological activity on its part, but as an awareness or prehension of that which is *received*. The theologian cannot designate revelation as an aspect of his method because he cannot say, "If you will proceed in a specified manner, revelation will take place." He can only assert that in the course of human inquiry and commitment such an awareness of ultimate meaning *has* been received. The prehension of this revelation, comparable with the apprehension of sensory perception and the comprehension of the principles of logical relationships, is appropriated rather than derived. The designation of an ultimate meaning for life, the determination of one rather than another of possible answers, rests not upon pure volition but upon a response to what has been presented. In this sense theology makes an appeal to authority in its determination.[16] It is "authoritative" because it is its own certification; it can appeal to no external criteria for validation.

The appropriation of revelation by the theologian is a basis of methodological activity rather than a part of it, in the same sense that the acceptance of sensory experience and discernment of logical relationships constitute the basis of empirical and rational judgments. One cannot empirically validate the acceptance of logical criteria nor rationally demonstrate the reliability of sensory experience. The certitude in each case calls for and permits no appeal beyond itself.

One word of caution must be inserted at this point. The revelation of ultimate meaning to which theology appeals as an authority does not afford it any authoritative determination of immediate and penultimate considerations. The imperialism of which theology has sometimes been guilty grows out of a misunderstanding at exactly this point. Revelation is neither an imparting of a formulated integration of all knowledge nor the providing of a "major premise" from which all elements of truth may be deductively derived. The manner in which theology seeks to draw knowledge of all sorts into an integrated and intelligible formulation with reference to this ultimate meaning is through human constructions, and though this formulation is the proper work of theology it does not claim authoritative significance.

The revelation to which theology appeals must be treated as *authoritative*. However, because like all forms of prehension it has its subjective pole, it need not be designated as *infallible*. "Perhaps the reality and worth of an authority which, for all its reality, is not the same thing as a formal inerrancy, is most readily illustrated from the sphere of moral life, a life which is more than merely natural and yet not fully and consciously supernatural. How impossible to maintain the inerrancy of a man's conscience, and yet how necessary to any serious morality to insist upon its authority! . . . I know that my conscience is not inerrant, but that knowledge does not excuse disobedience."[17] The unveiling of the ultimate meaning of life to which theology is committed, since its prehension involves subjective reference, cannot be posited as inerrant. Nonetheless, theology has no alternative to unswerving faithfulness to it.

The highly significant conversation in contemporary theology regarding the nature of revelation has been genuinely constructive. The emphases upon revelation "as self-disclosure *of* Person" as over against the notion of the impartation of information *about* Person, upon revelation as *acts* rather than *philosophical notions,* have distinct merit. Also, the insistence upon the fact that knowledge *of* Person involves some knowledge *about* Person is undeniable. It may well be, however, that the conversation, which often borders onto heated controversy, between the systematic and the Biblical theologian serves at times to obscure the more basic fact of the subjective, human reference which neither can escape.

When revelation is viewed in terms of *divine acts,* we are still faced with a condition of *act as witnessed and interpreted.* Historical event has subjective reference to whatever degree it is taken to have meaning. Similarly, if revelation be viewed as conceptual in character it stands as truth which is appropriate to, and structured by, characteristic human responses. Neither "event" nor "information" may be completely disjoined from the human manner of appropriation.

Rationalism in the Method of Theology

Because theology aspires to present truths which are more than tentative suggestions, because it undertakes to make affirmations which hold for all men under all circumstances, there is a natural recourse on the part of theology to turn eagerly to the principles of determination which are characteristic of logical inquiry. Another way of saying this is to recognize that the inclination toward absolute truth in any matter of ultimate concern imparts a special attractiveness to any program which undertakes to produce unquestionable affirmations.

There has persisted in theology a strong tendency toward pure rationalism, a fascination for the possibility of establishing the claims of religious truth upon necessary deductions from some limited number of axiomatic propositions. For theologians as well as philosophers the model of geometric reasoning has presented an ideal form of construction, a thoroughly consistent system the truths of which are incontrovertible in their derivation and universal in their appeal. There is no overstatement involved in asserting that the dominant apologetic function of theology has been essentially rationalistic, the effort to demonstrate that Christian affirmations are either required by reason or compatible with reason.

For its constructive task theology must place a necessary reliance in reason. This assertion involves no more than the obvious statement that theology employs a method which involves disciplined thinking rather than incoherent babbling. No appeal to extra-rational criteria absolves theology from the demand that its *formulations* be subject to the tests of consistency and order. "Religious truth must be developed from knowledge acquired when our ordinary senses and intellectual operations are at their highest pitch of discipline."[18] What Collingwood has to say about philosophy applies with equal force to theology: "There are some things which we can do without understanding what we are doing; not only things we do with our bodies, like locomotion and digestion, but even things we do with our minds, like making a poem or recognizing a face. But when that which we do is in the nature of thinking, it begins to be desirable, if we are to do it well, that we should understand what we are trying to do. . . . It is right to describe philosophic thought as deductive, because at every phase in its development it is, ideally at least, a complete system based on principles and connected throughout its texture by strict logical bonds; but the system is more than a deductive system, because the principles are open to criticism and must be defended by their success in explaining our experience."[19] In so far as the task of theology involves the intelligible presentation of truths it cannot avoid responsibility for rigorous rational formulation of its concepts. Only by consciously submitting its activity to the criticism of rationality can theology presume to claim that its work is genuinely subject to appropriation by the human mind.

The appropriate function of reason in theology can be indicated if it be kept in mind that theology incorporates philosophical speculation; that theology cannot be viewed as the product of rational construction, but rather as an activity which seeks to include rational constructions within its broader context. Specifically, this means that theology is called upon to indicate the inferences which may be drawn from the general affirmations of the Christian faith.[20] These inferences, if they are to be grasped and acknowledged, must be presented in propositional form. In the derivation and propositional formulation of such inferences theology must call upon the principles of logical analysis, and the principles employed are the same ones which operate in all areas of rational thought.

The function of reason for theology is limited to the determination of those formulated ideas which may be jointly held. In other words, reason presents one type of restriction upon theology; it serves to point to those statements which cannot be consistently affirmed in conjunction with certain other statements and to indicate what must necessarily follow *if certain rational constructions are taken to be true.* It cannot be contended that the exercise of rational processes will produce the truth regarding that which is of ultimate concern for men. The exercise of rationality can in no sense either vouch for or confirm the assertions of theology as a body of truth but only establish its coherence, or incoherence, *as a system.* What is indicated here with reference to the relationship of reason and theology only secondarily points to any feature of theology: primarily it is a description of the function of rational process. Rational construction and analysis nowhere provides anything more than an examination of the *relationship* between ideas. Theology is no special case. It receives neither more nor less service from rationality than does any other human inquiry. Reason serves to indicate not the ultimate truth or falsehood of theological affirmations but the logical relationship existing between two or more ideas; it can only establish whether or not a particular idea *as formulated* is consistent with some other idea.

If theology is a special case, its distinctiveness is to be found in the fact that there is some real question of whether or not the basic concepts of theological discourse are subject to logical formulation. This is not so much a question of whether certain Christian convictions are of human derivation or divine origin. It is the question as to whether these convictions, *however prehended,* can be *expressed* in unambiguous form. It is quite evident that for the sake of discourse theology must devise propositional forms for the concepts it employs. It is equally apparent that theology cannot afford to equate the propositions it constructs with the religious truths it seeks to convey. Every linguistic construction of basic theological import must be recognized as in some degree different from the truth it is intended to represent.[21] Accordingly, it is inappropriate for theology either to claim strict

Whitworth College Library
Spokane, Washington

validity for its inferences or to confine itself to those utterances which can be vindicated on purely rational grounds.

It is the reluctance to acknowledge that theological utterances are not necessarily strictly propositional which is at the root of certain unfortunate rationalistic and irrational emphases in theology. The most fantastic heresies of Christian history are the product of assuming that certain fundamental concepts are to be taken as literal equivalents of truth and following them through to their logical conclusions.[22] Emil Brunner warns, "For this very reason systematic unity, and logic pushed to an extreme, in the absolute sense of the word, are a sign of a false tendency in theological work."[23] The theologian who, in his zeal to claim the support of relentless logic for Christian affirmations, treats the formal statements of his faith as if they were rigorous logical propositions finds himself accomplishing an invalidation of his initial assumption by means of a *reductio ad absurdum*. Correspondingly, the irrationalist finds himself with no recourse except that of denying the essential reliability of a method which makes apparent the discrepancies which exist in his affirmations.

Quite obviously, theology as a form of discourse is forced to construct linguistic vehicles which are propositional in character. This is inherent in its task of making itself comprehensible. There is clear evidence, however, that in doing so it encounters logical inconsistencies. No theological system, however well thought out, has been able to avoid entirely a certain significant lack of coherence. This applies not only to subordinate inferences which may be drawn but to certain basic concepts which it seems impossible to formulate in such a way as to avoid direct contradiction. It hardly seems necessary to point to the frustration which has been produced by the various endeavors to phrase Christian convictions in such a manner that these contradictions can be resolved or explained away.

If the method of theology were unqualifiedly that of rational derivation and vindication, then it would be inescapably clear that such inconsistencies make its conclusions untenable. Actually, the critique of rationalism does something less than this. It does not brand theological conclusions as false, but it does make plain that theology cannot rest its claims upon its ability to offer a completely coherent view of life. If convictions which cannot be jointly held without inconsistency are incorporated within the same framework of knowledge and belief, then it must be on some basis other than reasonableness.

The acknowledgment of logical inconsistencies within a theological formulation leaves the way open for any one of several possible conclusions. One, of course, is that theology has thereby demonstrated its incompetence. Another possibility is the *tour de force* which endeavors to transmute this fundamental inconsistency into an argument for the supernatural truth which is involved. The appeal to absurdity is the most thoroughly fruitless device, however, which can be devised. In terms of such an aberration *The Hunting of the Snark* would far outweigh in theological significance Milton's effort to "assert eternal Providence, and justify the ways of God to men."[24] The more constructive and fruitful line of thought lies in recognizing that these inconsistencies simply call for an awareness that there is some lack of precise reference within the propositional forms of theological thought which demand caution in their manipulation. This is especially true with reference to the efforts which are sometimes made to draw significant inferences from contradictory formulations. In the process of theological work inconsistencies may be presented which lend themselves to no genuine resolution.

In such a case it may be necessary to recognize them for what they are, but no further conclusion may be drawn from them.

There is no brilliance of intellect involved in reaching some startling observation from the joint assertion of contradictions. From P and not-P, Q follows.[25] I may feel that any adequate Christian theology contains the joint assertions of God's sovereignty and of man's freedom. I undertake to assert, "It is true that God completely determines each act of His creatures," and, "It is not true that God completely determines each act of His creatures" (if that is not what I intend by "sovereignty" and "freedom," then it is incumbent upon me to specify what I do mean), and draw from this the assertion that "therefore each man is responsible to God for his own acts." The conclusion which has been drawn *may* be *true*. It is formally *valid* in the sense that it follows from the previous propositions. The catch is that any other statement, true or false, can be derived with exactly the same logical force. *As a matter of formal validity* we may assert that "therefore God is seven feet, three inches tall" or "all triangles have seven sides." Once I have introduced into my line of reasoning two propositions, one of which is the contradiction of the other, and assert both of them to be true, then I have created the logical chaos in which the conditions exist for asserting the truth of every proposition. It is entirely possible to engage in a fruitful sort of dialectical reasoning in which irreconcilable elements are recognized and expressed. However, these irreconcilable elements may not be formulated and treated as contradictory propositions without creating logical anarchy.

The presence of the paradoxical element in Christian truth has come in for a considerable degree of discussion within the present century. The glorification of the paradox is frequently nothing more than a euphemism, a delusion that by calling an inconsistency by some other name we manage to overcome its offensiveness. In such an event the game of playing paradox bears witness to the exhaustion of the fundamental ideas involved and represents a mere going through the motions of thinking.[26] The paradoxes of Zeno did not prove that the Ionians were wrong nor the Eleatics right. They simply witnessed to the fact that the cosmological speculations of early Greek thought could not move farther without some new insights, mathematical or ontological.

There are at least two senses in which the term "paradox" is employed. The most basic familiar meaning of the word refers to a literary device consciously introduced for the sake of suggesting conceptual overtones which escape more literal and straightforward discourse. This is an entirely appropriate and effective linguistic form of poetic communication which relies upon startling incongruity of statement to point to the complexity of the human situation, or to suggest the element of surprise which contributes to the enjoyment of life. The effect of this device rests in large measure upon the equivocal reference of certain terms such that language can suggest meanings which are not distinctly expressed. There is no basis for objecting to the presence of this form of expression in the realm of theology. The Scriptures and the writings of Augustine and Kierkegaard abound with such utterances. They serve well to arrest the attention and to demand some aesthetic as well as cognitive response. The "literary paradox" is linguistic in character. It is presumed that the "contradiction" is only apparent and that it would disappear if the same cognitive content were re-expressed in more literal language.

Existentialist thought, Christian and non-Christian, has focused attention upon another sense in which we may look at the paradox. Here we are presented with the paradox which is something more than a literary device or linguistic oddity. Within this context there is a protest against idealistic philosophy which identifies the "rational" and the "real," an insistence that any type of construction which forces the unsystematic realities of existence into the neat categories of conception does so only by a serious distortion. Consequently the paradox is viewed not so much as a conscious poetic construction as a reflection in language of the fundamentally non-systematic and irrational character of existence. Kierkegaard makes full use of the literary function of paradoxical construction, but he goes far beyond this in intent and force. The quality of uniqueness in each "self," the unanticipated and unrestricted nature of divine activity, and the nonobjective quality of truth all point to the contradictions which must inevitably arise out of any endeavor to "draw them with the net" of any formalized description.

It is the recognition of this second and more significant sort of paradox which is essential for the exercise of rationalistic methods and critique in theology. The presence of logical inconsistency is endemic with theology, pathological in the sense that it is indicative of the basic impossibility of confining divine activity and human existence within the static limits of logical constructions. For the sake of intelligibility in communication theology is compelled to employ the rational constructions which make discourse possible. This means that it must ordinarily present statements which are propositional in form and subject to the rigorous critique of logic. It pays a high price, however, for securing this basis of communication. Whenever carried beyond the most superficial level this rational process reveals bare and disturbing inconsistencies. Theology must employ rational technique in seeking to examine the inferences of the basic truths it affirms, but it need not be surprised that in doing so it encounters stark contradictions.

Stated briefly, it would seem that rational construction and critique must occupy an important place in theological work. For the sake of communication it has no choice but to employ logical forms and analysis. However, because of the impossibility of reducing its basic affirmations to strict propositional form, theology must not suppose that it can turn itself into a genuinely rational system. If its basic affirmations are mistakenly assumed to be genuine propositions, then its work is invalidated by the presence of inescapable contradictions. If its basic affirmations are acknowledged to be propositional only in form and not in the sense of clear and unequivocal reference, then theology must view with caution all subordinate inferences which are drawn from them.[27] In other words, the presence of inconsistency or paradox, call it what you will, within the basic structure of theology does not serve to invalidate theology but does serve to indicate that the rational formulations of theology must have the limited function of making possible communication, rather than the extensive function of strict certification.

Experiential Reference in the Method of Theology

From the conclusions already advanced concerning the scope and method of theology it may be readily inferred that theology must *participate* in some degree in the type of knowledge which is oriented to human sensory experience, but that such knowledge cannot serve as the sole basis for theological construction and apologetic. In its interpretation of physical phenomena theology, like natural science, has no starting point except as it appeals to that data which is transmitted by the senses. In so far as theology must incorporate that knowledge of the natural world which is relevant for ultimate determinations—and any such knowledge may well prove to be relevant—it must rely upon the public and verifiable information of sensory character. It is possible to acknowledge that in the accumulation and interpretation of such knowledge theology is dependent upon scientific procedure. It should be readily apparent that for its work theology is concerned that the sensory knowledge which it incorporates shall be the most accurate available. Accordingly it employs the method determined by the subject matter under investigation.

There is no occasion for theology to be suspicious of or condescending toward experiential knowledge. The seriousness with which the Christian faith take the historical setting of its message gives particular relevance to all reality which is witnessed to by the experience of men. "God cannot enter the stream of time except in definite and conditioned relation to history, and that truth can come to man only as an element in conscious experience and as related to human life."[28] The heritage of Christianity is to look upon sensory experience neither as irrelevant nor as essentially deceptive but as the basis for the understanding of the natural order of being.

In the description and interpretation of sensory experience theology must function scientifically. That is not to say that the whole theological enterprise is a science, or that the recognized procedures of science furnish for theology its essential method. The dominance of empirical epistemology and the growing prestige of the natural sciences during the past few centuries have produced some inclination to assert the scientific character of theology, even to seek to establish it as a science. The "spirit of the age" is such that if the theologian desired to commend his conclusions to the mind of modern Western man he felt called upon to justify his affirmations in terms of some empirical epistemology. It was this consideration which led D. C. MacIntosh to feel that Christian truth could best commend itself to the twentieth century by establishing its scientific justification, and that "if theology is to become really scientific it must be by becoming fundamentally empirical."[29]

There is significant value in calling attention to the fact that sensory experience occupies a dominant place in furnishing us with the basis of certitude and in exercising a critical judgment on our theoretical constructions. It is extremely difficult for the human mind to give serious and persisting assent to formulations which are not consistent with experiential evidence. Certain religious convictions may have their initial claim based upon ecclesiastical pronouncements or traditional formulations. "But however they may have entered into one's theological theory, they are held consistently with the ideal of a scientific theology if they are held subject to progressive verification or refutation by having their logical consequences examined in the light of the facts of experience."[30] There is no way of anticipating the tenacity with which some individual or group may hold to a formulation which is contrary to the evidence of the senses, but the negative judgment of experience makes it impossible for such a belief to persist in the general thinking of mankind.

The judgment of the senses exercises this negative control on theology, and the scientific investigation of phenomena is theology's only reliable means of interpreting empirical data. This does not mean, however, that theology is to view its function as scientific in the sense that it limits its affirmations to those which are derived from sensory evidence or rejects all concepts except those which are empirically vindicated. Empirical knowledge makes up only a part of theological concern, a significant part for which it must rely upon scientific determinations. But theology must undertake to consider evidence and insights which are not empirical in character but which are distinctly relevant in ultimate deter-

minations. Accordingly, scientific methodology is not adequate for the evaluation of this non-empirical data or for
effecting an integration which must incorporate non-sensory
but relevant prehensions.

The chief example of non-sensory data which is of concern
to theology is the form of insight, still properly designated as
experiential, which is not "public," quantitative, or subject
to strict empirical description. In this category we must include both those forms of "religious experience" which are of
fairly general nature, supposedly possible for all sensitive
individuals, and the less general "mystical insights" which
are confined to a very few persons. Theology must give serious
attention to those general human responses, ordinarily
recognized as belonging to the province of the psychology of
religion, which make it possible for there to be some communication of insights. It must be prepared, also, to view
with interest the recounted experience of the mystic. These
are forms of *experience,* non-sensory to be sure, which are
ordinarily described by analogy to sensory responses.[31] The
fact that these experiences, whether of fairly general or somewhat unique character, are heavily weighed on the side of
subjectivity does not detract from their significance for theology. In its inclusive function it must be prepared to give
proper weight to these "private" experiences as well as to
"public" ones.

Theology need make no prohibitive judgments regarding
the possibility of unique illumination or intuition on the part
of some individual. In fact, the characteristic appeal of organ-
ized religion to the normative significance of certain private
experiences, accorded revelatory importance, presupposes the
authenticity of at least some of these insights. For the mystic
himself there is no type of evidence which surpasses, or even
approaches, in compelling certitude the direct vividness of

his own prehension of ultimate reality. The fact that it is vague in cognitive content, that it is acknowledged as inexpressible, militates against its carrying corresponding conviction for anyone else. For the individual involved, however, it stands as the criterion against which all other impressions and judgments are measured.

The significance of private experiences for theology rests upon the possibility of discerning the elements of these experiences which find some counterpart in the responses of a community. Theology can employ them only to the degree that they find some responsive affirmation at the level of more general religious experience. Because it must speak for and to the Church, theology must endeavor to translate that which is unique into some form of universal categories. In doing so it may, perforce, sacrifice much which it would like to convey, but the demands of discourse make such a sacrifice inevitable.

In this respect theology simply employs the critical discernment which it shares with science and philosophy. In all human inquiries there are intuitional aspects of discovery, insights which occur to some one individual. They are authenticated, however, or at least made available to other individuals, only to the degree that they can find some form of confirmation within general experience. Russell writes in this connection: "Of the reality or unreality of the mystic's world I know nothing. I have no wish to deny it, or even to declare that the insight which reveals it is not a genuine insight. What I do wish to maintain—and it is here that the scientific attitude become imperative—is that insight, untested and unsupported, is an insufficient guarantee of truth, in spite of the fact that much of the most important truth is first suggested by its means. . . . Instinct, intuition, or insight is what first leads to the beliefs which subsequent reason confirms or confutes; but the confirmation, where it is possible, consists, in the last analysis, of agreement with other beliefs no less instinctive. Reason is a harmonizing, controlling force rather than a creative one. Even in the most purely logical realms, it is insight that first arrives at what is new. . . . It is true that intuition has a convincingness which is lacking to intellect: while it is present, it is almost impossible to doubt its truth. But if it should appear, on examination, to be at least as fallible as intellect, its greater subjective certainty becomes a demerit, making it only the more irresistibly deceptive."[32]

In order to do justice to the broader concerns of theology every weight must be given to the unique awareness of the individual. However, in order to speak to the community it represents, theology must endeavor to set this unique experience within a more general context. It must examine these unique insights in terms of general experience *of the same order*. It is not called upon to subject the non-sensory experiences to empirical verification, but it must seek to find the common elements of subjective response which are characteristic of mankind. Only by so doing may it appropriate the insight of the mystic. In this sense we may say that theology relies upon the confirmatory evidence of experience. Only as insights elicit some validating confirmation in the response of the community to which a communication of it is directed can theology incorporate them within its work.[33]

The experiential reference of theology, its necessary reference to that data which is strictly empirical and to that which is non-sensory, makes appropriate to its method the appeal to whatever public awareness or private insight it may employ in construction or criticism. For its acquisition of knowledge of the physical world it is dependent upon the same empirical and inductive determinations that constitute the approach of natural science. However, since its scope includes the non-sensory experiences and responses of individuals, it cannot presume to limit its affirmations to those which are subject to empirical verification. Such an approach is not adequate for its comprehensive task. The negative criticisms of empirical investigation must carry significant, though not conclusive, weight. Formulations of theology which are controverted by empirical evidence must, to say the least, be viewed with suspicion. Some evidence of a different order must be present to justify an affirmation which is controverted by empirical facts.[34] Empirical methodology cannot serve as the essential constructive approach of theology except as it furnishes significant data regarding the nature of the physical world. It does, however, serve as a critical reference at all points where the affirmations of theology impinge upon the world of sense experience.

Volitional Reference in the Method of Theology

The method of theology incorporates for its constructions and critiques rational and empirical techniques which are in no significant degree different from the employment of them in science and philosophy. In fact, the scientific and philosophical applications of logical and empirical determination properly fall within the more comprehensive scope of theological concern. In whatever degree the subject matter under consideration makes possible the criticism of rational consistency or of empirical confirmation the conclusions of theology are derived and tested by the appropriate methodology. The criteria of reason and experience are relevant for the formation of theological judgments, even though they may not be accorded final value.

In the effort to produce the certitude which is appropriate for theology, however, these two methods do not stand alone.

The appeal to some form of authority has already been introduced as distinctive of theology, as applicable in a sense in which it does not appear in science and philosophy (pp. 105 ff.). Theology must give primary consideration to a form of certitude which rests upon a determination of ultimate meaning which has been "given" rather than empirically or rationally derived. The designation, description, and appropriation of this "given," this Revelation, is the distinctive and most difficult aspect of theological method.

The reference which theology makes to authority cannot be through an objectifying of either the content or the form of its revelation. To some extent it is objectified, made available, through the form it is witnessed to by the community for which theology speaks. But even when this is recognized, the subjective pole of revelation cannot be ignored. Herein lies the greater comprehensiveness of theology; it may consciously and deliberately include that relevant and inescapable subjectivity which is present in all forms of certitude but which both science and philosophy must seek to eliminate or ignore. The terms "revelation" and "authority" are relational terms; revelation for someone, authority for someone.

When we assert that theology incorporates an appeal to authority which is not appropriate for science or philosophy, we are also pointing to the fact that a subjective determination is involved. The revelation which is essential to theological activity involves an appropriation or reception of it by some self.[35] The according to it of authoritative significance involves some act of personal choice and commitment inseparable from the authority which is posited.[36] An authority is authoritative because someone acknowledges it as such, because of a volitional determination. Its status is not determined by rational or empirical demonstration. If that were the case it would be something less than genuine authority.

Similarly, revelation carries with it its appropriate certitude because of a volitional determination. If its status depended upon rational or empirical verification, it would be something less than revelation. There is nothing which necessitates its force except the choice involved.

In calling attention to this volitional aspect in theology there is no intent to indicate that it relies upon arbitrary and capricious choice. As has already been stressed (pp. 103 ff.) any significant and meaningful choice must be between genuine alternatives. At this point both reason and experience serve to restrict in some measure those choices which seem to be genuine possibilities. Having acknowledged the importance of this restriction, theology must accord realistic consideration to the *hairetic* element in its methodology.[37] The determination of authority or the designation of revelation involves a decision which is not itself a rational or empirical judgment.

Hairetic and non-cognitive judgments appear as essential parts of all constructive systems. They may be defined and recognized but not eliminated. Science finds it necessary to accept certain non-scientific modes of justification, decisions based on aesthetic or utilitarian grounds.[38] It must introduce the criteria of "elegance" or "simplicity" in selecting one from a number of plausible explanations of phenomena. On empirical evidence alone there is no basis for asserting the superiority of the Copernican system over the Ptolemaic. If one is content to introduce literally hundreds of *ad hoc* modifications to take care of the observed variations from the original Ptolemaic construction, the motions of the heavenly bodies can be quite well accounted for under the older system. It is the elegance or simplicity of the heliocentric theory which makes it "superior" to the geocentric. The constancy of the speed of light for any frame of reference is not a dictum which can be derived or confirmed by observation. The theories of relativity which are based upon the dictum commend themselves for scientific acceptance not because they are the only possible context of explanation but because they offer the most elegant and fruitful theoretical formulation. One may quite well maintain that the speed of light is a variable if he is willing to undertake the fantastic adjustments of special and temporal calculations which would be required. Even logical systems require non-logical and subjectively oriented determinations. There is no logical superiority of a system with three axioms over a system with five hundred axioms. An aesthetic appeal is introduced. Ockham's razor, "entia non sunt multiplicanda praeter necessitatem," has been an effective tool of all critical philosophy. It is the expression, however, of a decision which rests upon no logical or experiential necessity. It is dictated by the same predilection toward simplicity which motivates scientific choices. The individual preferences which color the conclusions of any philosopher, scientist, or theologian may be obscured or cancelled out by other accidental features, but there persists the inevitable element of volitional determination.

Theology endeavors to frame answers regarding man's ultimate question. Consequently, it cannot operate without drawing into its considerations whatever is of significance for man, and certainly his choices and responses are of major significance. There is no possibility of ignoring the subjective determinations which make up a large part of existence. When Whitehead writes, "It is more important that a proposition be interesting than that it be true,"[39] he has no wish to minimize the place of logical coherence and empirical verification. He is pointing to the fact that the capacity to elicit some response is of more consequence for a statement than its formal veracity. Nothing is more precise, or less significant, than an exact tautology. A proposition, even a false one, is significant if it serves to stimulate some response. Kierkegaard tells the story of the inmate who escapes from an asylum and determines to act in such a way that everyone will regard him as completely sane. Acting upon the assumption that a sane person is one who will talk in a manner that everyone will recognize to be objectively true, he seeks to be entirely objective. He places a ball in his coat pocket and walks through the village slapping his pocket and announcing to all he meets, "The world is round." He was somewhat disturbed that people could not recognize his objective pronouncements as evidence of his sanity.

Theology may not cut itself off from objective truth; it may not disregard the objective determinations of reason and experience. However, it cannot deal with ultimate concern unless it takes into its considerations the choices which men must make. For this reason theology regards the subjective responses of individuals not as some shameful interloper which must be kept out of sight, but as a welcomed context which imparts meaning to propositions which cannot be couched in purely objective terms. This is what Santayana means when he contends that art and religion can employ "imagination" and "passionate understanding" for the sake of relevant truths which are not accessible to detached rationality. "The imagination, therefore, must furnish to religion and to metaphysics those large ideas tinctured with passion . . . Thus the stone which the builder, understanding, rejected, becomes the chief stone of the corner; the intuitions which science could not use remain the inspiration of poetry and religion. . . . The imagination, when thus employed to anticipate or correct the conclusions of the understanding, is of course not called imagination by those who appeal to it. The religious teachers call it prophecy or revelation, the philosophers call it a higher reason. But these names are merely eulogistic synonyms for imagination."[40] One may argue about the propriety of designating this as imagination, or about the correctness of proclaiming that "these large ideas tinctured with passion" are the *chief* stone of the theological enterprise. Theology, however, cannot build without it.

The hairetic determinations involved in theology need to be recognized for what they are. In fact, so far as method itself is concerned, that is about all that theology can do with them. It can neither derive them by other means nor vindicate them on other grounds. They exist as choices. Theology may point to them and seek to express them in the clearest and most comprehensible form, but it cannot alter their fundamental nature.

The extent and variety of these hairetic determinations are too great to permit a detailed description. In part they are the reflection of those particular circumstances and reactions which are the accidental characteristics of individuals or groups. But when we have explained conditioning factors in the setting of a choice, we have not reduced the choice to something of a different order. The Lutheran emphasis upon a faith which is essentially a trust in the goodness of God, an emphasis which becomes a criterion for all other theological considerations, can be substantiated by appeal to Scripture and to Christian tradition. However, the vividness of Luther's own experience of transition from paralyzing fear to joyous trust must be recognized as a subjective reference which imparts meaning to his theological formulations. The fact that the Apostle Paul has had a similar experience and the fact that Luther's message met with a ready response from the hearts of his hearers constitutes a verification which is itself subjective rather than objective.

The same thing might be observed with reference to the priority given by Calvin to the doctrine of election. It has its strong exegetical support, but the significance of the doctrine is not to be expressed in terms of deductions from Scripture alone. The emphasis on the will of God as the sole determinant of salvation was a way of meeting the spiritual blackmail involved in claiming for ecclesiastical authorities the power of deciding the ultimate fate of individuals.

Decisions are made; choices are accepted. That these determinations involve subjective preferences and wishes is to say nothing one way or the other about the objective truth of the constructions. They are not made as the result of detachment, but by way of involvement. Whatever criterion of *truth* may be applied, they are clearly *significant*.

A number of the hairetic determinations of theology are so general in acceptance that it is sometimes easy to mistake them for logical necessities. It is difficult to see how theology would function apart from some presupposition of purpose within the cosmic scene. Hume contended that no type of evidence could be advanced to establish the presence of cause or purpose within the realm of nature. In this he seems to be correct. Yet for all thinking, theological and non-theological, some such assumption is so general as to appear to be a necessary truth. There is for science an emotional abhorrence of chaos. Order, like purpose, is presupposed on subjective grounds rather than established by objective methods.[41] For theology there is the same rejection of purposelessness; not because purpose is logically necessary but because it is the only fruitful presupposition. We have not altered the picture if we suggest that theology stands in a special position because the truth of purpose has come by revelation. There still exists the fact of the choosing of that particular revelation of purpose.

It would obviously be trivial for theology to undertake to

make hairetic determinations the only appropriate elements in procedure. It cannot assert that something is so simply because someone, or everybody, would wish it to be that way. Human decision between genuine possibilities is not the only aspect of reality, but it is a significant aspect of reality. Sometimes the only way of imparting meaning to what we affirm is to put it in the form, "This is how I am determined to act." Even where the particular line of action may not receive general approval there is an appeal to a common element of intelligibility and understanding.

Hairetic determination in theology is no substitute for other means of determination, even as no other method may be substituted for it. Where it is present, it calls for frank recognition of its nature. Ordinarily it may be said to occupy an important place at "both ends" of the theological enterprise. It is involved in the designation of those choices which are both logically and chronologically prior to all thinking. It appears again in those situations where it becomes necessary to choose between alternatives, and where the exercise of reason and experience can serve to do no more than delimit the area of choice.

Convergence as the Integrating Method of Theology

In reaching conclusions at various levels of certitude theology is called upon to employ not one method but several. For construction and for criticism it must rely upon the same logic and empirical investigation which are within the province of science and philosophy. In addition it must apply the method of hairetic determination (if it may be called a method), must recognize the choices which men make and which theology itself must make. No one of these, however, will serve to unify the broad scope of theology into a comprehensive pattern nor to integrate the whole toward a determination of ultimate meaning.

One of the most marked tendencies of reflective thinking, a tendency motivated by the pervasive desire for unity and simplicity, has been to discover some single method of determination of truth which will be applicable to the whole range of human concern. Frequently men have felt that they have laid hold of some such talisman, that they have found some fruitful method of inquiry which may be indefinitely extended.

It is not difficult to sense the optimism of the Pythagoreans who, discovering the applicability of arithmetic notations for diverse aspects of experience, concluded that in "number" they had found the key which would open every lock. It is easy to understand how an insight into the connection existing between language and thought can lead to the aspiration to find in the structure of language the means of laying hold of the secrets of cognition itself. For generation after generation the elegance and certitude of geometric demonstration has led philosophers to seek to extend the method of geometry to all areas of inquiry. Plato, Descartes, Leibnitz, Spinoza, among others, sought for a universal mathematics or calculus which would enable them to reduce all the diverse opinions of mankind to a few certain truths. The success which came from submitting one field after another to the scrutiny of empirical generalization prompted scientific philosophers to trust that all mysteries of the universe might be made subject to positivistic description. A mode of investigation which could reduce the atom and the galaxy into the same laws of force ought to be able to encompass the whole range of being. The theologian can become absorbed with the realization that God has communicated something to man which he could not

hope to discover for himself. He may be led thereby to conclude that the particular form or content of this communication becomes the only reliable way of knowledge.

The successful application of a method of investigation in a
limited field may quite properly lead to an effort to learn just
how far it may be extended without loss of reliability. The
danger lies in the arbitrary imposition of a method upon any
and all realms of knowledge. It is against this type of imposition that Tillich warns: "Method and system determine each
other. Therefore, no method can claim to be adequate for
every subject. Methodological imperialism is as dangerous as
political imperialism; like the latter, it breaks down when the
independent elements of reality revolt against it. A method is
not an 'indifferent net' in which reality is caught, but method
is an element of the reality itself."[42]

Imperialism of this sort has been attempted by theology no
less than by science or philosophy. The effort has been made
to enthrone one way of knowing as the only possible way, to
prescribe not only method but the particular conclusions
which may be drawn. This effort can only result in a breakdown of all communication.

This problem comes into sharp focus as we raise the question of how theology can attempt to integrate its own insights
and the conclusions of philosophy and science. It may share
with all other disciplines the logical and empirical standards which are appropriate for the examination of the world
of physical realities and conceptual constructions. It may,
further, have its own appeal to revelation and subjective response in the effort to understand that which lies outside the
range of science and philosophy. But in what fashion does
theology propose to effect a coherent structure of knowledge
which has been derived by various means and tested in various
ways? Further, is there any way by which it can produce an

integration of truth and at the same time avoid the imperial-ism of imposing upon particular branches of inquiry a set of criteria which is inappropriate?

The integration which theology effects must be one which does not prescribe the conclusions of empirical investigation or impose imperialistic restrictions upon rational speculation and analysis. It must, therefore, be of such nature that it is not entirely foreign to the processes of thought which are characteristic of the subordinate disciplines. This can be ac-complished if we keep in mind the fact that certitude in all realms of knowledge is ordinarily not produced by exclusive reliance upon a single formal, rigorous procedure to the ex-clusion of all other considerations. Rather, in all significant forms of inquiry there are incorporated elements of logical, empirical, and hairetic determination.

The comprehensive method of theology, the means by which it seeks to draw its particular contributions and those of subordinate disciplines into some ordered whole, is simply the ordinary process of cumulative thinking, difficult to de-scribe with exactness but productive of that form of certitude which furnishes the basis of most of our practical decision. We are all accustomed in reaching decisions to say, or at least to think, "Well, all things considered, this seems to be the answer." We certainly haven't considered *all things* in reach-ing the decision, but we are indicating that having taken into consideration such relevant and significant data *of all orders* as we have at hand, we are prepared to draw some conclusion. We see some convergence of evidence from different quarters, in-formally combine and weigh the different types of presupposi-tions and inclinations which affect us, and reach a final judg-ment which cannot be identified with any one intellectual or cognitive process.

Several attempts to describe this most general sort of thinking may be cited. H. F. Rall writes: "Knowing is not a special activity or 'faculty' of man; it is an aspect of the total process of living."[43] D. C. MacIntosh presents a similar emphasis: *"The burden of proof lies upon those who would substitute for the fundamentals of the common-sense point of view any doctrine which is foreign to those ways of thinking which have borne and still bear the test of universal human practice."*[44] It is what L. H. DeWolf designates as *comprehensive coherence*: "One of the commonest meanings of reason and also one of the most highly commended in philosophical circles is the process of examining an idea or object in the widest possible context of thought and experience. He who uses the reason of comprehensive coherence will accept as most probably true that proposed solution of a problem which is, on the whole, supported by the greatest net weight of evidence from all quarters. It is assumed that the truth is not actually contradicted by experience nor by other truth and that we can have evidence of the truth of an idea only through its significant relation to some experience. . . . The reason of comprehensive coherence seems the most adequate rational instrument for discerning truth."[45]

Philosophers and theologians alike turn to some expression of convergence of complex lines of inquiry as the source of practical certitude. This is indicated by Hans Reichenbach. "A physical theory is a rather complex aggregate; its different components may have different probabilities which should be determined separately. The probabilities occurring here are not all of the same level."[46] Writing from an entirely different philosophical orientation Santayana suggests: "I think that common sense, in a rough dogged way, is technically sounder than the special schools of philosophy, each of which squints and overlooks half the facts and half the difficulties in its eagerness to find in some detail the key to the whole."[47] In his discussion of the *method of correlation* Tillich presents as the fundamental tool of theology this same sort of comprehensive thought which is somewhat less specific in procedure than are its component elements: "Systematic theology uses the method of correlation. It has always done so, sometimes more, sometimes less, consciously, and must do so consciously and outspokenly, especially if the apologetic point of view is to prevail. The method of correlation explains the contents of the Christian faith through existential questions and theological answers in mutual interdependence."[48]

The convergence of evidence toward a unified judgment in theology is most closely akin to the unanalyzed conclusions of common-sense decision. By an informal process pertinent subordinate conclusions are drawn to an integration through a general evaluation which is not peculiarly that of any one of the methods which have produced the contributory evidence. In those ordinary decisions which are necessitated by living we are accustomed to drawing upon a complex of logical, empirical, aesthetic, traditional, and hairetic determinations for the sake of a concrete decision which cannot be identified with any one of the component parts. In this same manner theology effects an integration of diverse judgments, not by reliance upon any one of them but upon their general convergence.

The most important appeal of theology is not to any one of the contributory methods of inquiry but to the informal procedure of ordinary thought. In theology, as in any other convergent judgment, no fixed scale can be established for the relative weight of different orders of knowledge. The empirical impression that an arrow is in motion will outweigh even the most persuasive rationalization of Zeno, whether or not the paradox receives rational resolution. On the other hand, the rational certainty of an arithmetic relationship is such that if one sees five apples placed on a table and three more added to them, if he observes six apples there, he literally does not believe his senses; he is confident that some sleight-of-hand has been involved. A single celestial observation will serve to refute the most scholarly reasoning to prove that there can be no change outside the orbit of the moon. An intuitive certainty of a man's honesty may outweigh all circumstantial evidence to the contrary.

Similarly, there is for theology no single appeal which will be normative in every circumstance. Scriptural evidence may be accorded greater weight than any emotional revulsion against the idea of eternal punishment. A single experience of prayer may carry a greater conviction than any marshalling of rational evidences for the immutability of God, or even of a number of experiences of futile prayer. Double predestination may be conceded to be completely logical and still be rejected within a broader context of truth.

There do occur those rare significant judgments in which all evidence, logical, traditional, empirical, seems to point toward a single conclusion. In these cases a condition of certitude exists not because of any one single line of evidence but because of the convergence of them. In other cases the evidences which point away from a conclusion may be slight. However, theology encounters a number of problems for which various kinds of subordinate judgments are relevant and in which there is genuine divergence of evidence. In such an event theology cannot safely *disregard* any of the elements which make the decision difficult and complex. It must, however, *while regarding them,* form some integrating judgment. This is the sort of thinking upon which we rely from day to day in all affairs of life. It is of the essence of common sense.

A number of the rather commonly agreed-upon conclusions of Christian theologians are the product not of specifically empirical, authoritative, or rational approach but of an informal combination of various types of thinking. Evangelical theologians will generally agree that there are two sacraments, two ecclesiastical acts which have a special significance for the Church. This decision is hardly a strict empirical judgment. It may be experiential in part in the sense that a large number of Christians testify that these two acts have special meaningfulness to them. However, the experiential evidence is not conclusive. Individuals will testify to having felt far more religious overtone associated with their marriage than with their baptism. It can hardly be held that this is a Scripturally authoritative determination. Certainly foot-washing would have Scriptural basis as an additional sacrament. Tradition alone does not answer the question. Rather there is a decision based upon tradition, Scripture, subjective response. It is a matter of "all things considered—."

Similarly, the judgment which the theologian may reach with regard to divorce is the product not simply of Scriptural exegesis, or of empirical sociological evidence, or of rational analysis, or of personal bias, or of a direct and personal guidance by the Holy Spirit. Again it is a matter of "all things considered—." Decisions must be made, and it is rare in serious decisions that all contributory evidence points in the same direction. Yet the process of ordinary thought makes possible some combination of evidence.

In attributing to theology the integrating method of "common sense" with its honorific connotation, we must also acknowledge its inherent limitation. Common sense certainly can lay no claim to infallibility. We rely upon it not because it is flawless but because it is necessary. The convergence of evidence, except in rare instances, tends to be in an "area" rather than at a "point." There does not exist the precision which we would like to have. It would be extremely helpful if there existed some super-calculus whereby we could assign relative weight to different orders of evidence, but unfortunately we are dealing with incommensurables. We must *combine* factors which we cannot *add*. We must *integrate* judgments which we cannot even *reduce* to the same categories. In order to do this we experience a surrender of that specificity which remains possible so long as we have confined our attention to a single form of knowledge.

In almost all types of thinking, precision is inversely related to breadth of concern. The logician may move with greatest assurance when he limits himself to symbols which are devoid of specific reference. Psychological and sociological constructions are exact only when abstracted from existing situations. Theology deliberately chooses to extend its scope and concern literally to the ultimate. It can do so only by some sacrifice of the rigor and exactitude which would be possible if it chose a more limited field.

Recognizing this limitation, it is only fair to exercise caution in attributing terms of "truth" or "knowledge" to theological constructions. Although there is some qualification in the manner in which these terms should be used, there is no need to qualify the use of the terms "certitude" and "meaningfulness." Because theology undertakes to "combine incommensurables" it is not surprising that the convergence of evidence may not be of the same order as one or another of the constituent parts. Because *subjective* reactions have been frankly acknowledged as a significant element in this convergence it is not surprising that a point of convergence cannot be *objectively* demonstrated. Yet it is still possible to maintain that the affirmations of theology have genuine *meaning*. If that meaning is *less precise* than the analytic philosopher would demand, it is also considerably more inclusive *and more significant*. Specifically, the conscious reference to choice and decision as a form of determination imparts to theological conclusions one of the most readily recognizable definitions of "meaning": "This is the manner in which I propose to act."

Setting aside for the moment the supposedly objective terms "truth" and "knowledge," it is possible to focus attention upon "certitude" as a state of mind which permits unqualified disposition to act. This is both the aim and the accomplishment of theology. It is quite in order to suggest that such certitude is something not "lower" but "higher" than knowledge. The theological integration effected by the convergence of different orders of knowledge cannot presume to produce a knowledge which is identical in reference with some one element within it. It points rather to that sort of determination which involves choices and is itself of the order of choice.

There is no need to suppose that theology is in a position to elicit a conviction which is devoid of subjective reference. It would be denying its comprehensive concern were it to aim at that. The conviction it seeks to produce is none the less definite. Tentativeness is entirely appropriate to detached judgments. The involvement of theological determinations precludes tentativeness. In its strongest expression it is not dissimilar to what Descartes describes by "intuition," when he insists that each new step in a line of inquiry calls for a "re-intuiting" of the whole. The entire process of determination is brought back into focus in terms of the ultimate concern of man.

Method in Construction, Critique, and Apologetic

The method of theology is its means of appropriating the significant conclusions of the less inclusive disciplines and of employing them in an effort to define and describe man's ultimate meaning and objective. For a method it cannot simply appropriate and extend any one of the contributory methods. These it uses in the same manner and subject to the same critiques as do the other inquiries it seeks to incorporate. For the integration of the whole it must rely upon the less precise approach of common-sense convergence of diverse forms of understanding.

As a means of construction it proceeds in the description and explanation of physical phenomena in basically the same manner as does science. In fact, it may find it entirely satisfactory to "rely upon science" as a different discipline to undertake this specific task. In accepting and using the results of scientific inquiry, theology is not disqualifying itself to speak in matters of empirical knowledge, nor is it expressing lack of concern in the scientific enterprise. Rather, it is following the practical procedure of appropriating the best available insight as it comes from those people most familiar with a particular form of investigation. In the same manner it draws inferences from general concepts by exactly the same rational methodology as does the logician. It knows of no special rules of consistency. Its method of integration can be said to be its own only in the sense that every person is engaging in a *theological* enterprise when he attempts to bring his whole range of knowledge and experience to a focus in an effort to reach some ultimate determination.

It has already been contended that any specified method must include its own critique. The method of derivation must also serve as the means of criticism. So far as logical and empirical determinations in theology are concerned, no special situation exists. To the extent that the theologian calls upon logical demonstrations and empirical judgments those conclusions are subject to the appropriate criteria. His logical inferences must meet the test of consistency. His judgments concerning the physical world are subject to the verification or refutation of sensory experience. With reference to the soundness of the integration effected it would seem that one test is applicable. It must be in terms of the "certitude" which it aspires to produce. The appropriate question is, "Does this formulation produce a state of certitude which leads me to an unqualified commitment of myself to it?"

In its apologetic function theology must seek formulations which coincide with experience and which are expressed in a manner to preserve as high a degree of internal consistency as is possible. It cannot avoid an appeal to those determinations which are non-objective, but in doing so it must frankly acknowledge the hairetic elements. It may not assume that those choices will be uniformly made, and consequently cannot presume that its conclusions which involve them will find universal acceptance, but it can thereby make its affirmations intelligible.

Although there are no theoretical limits to the concern of theology, there do exist certain practical limits which must be recognized and acknowledged. Theology cannot free itself from the limitations imposed by the nature of language which serves as its vehicle of communication, by the subjective reference which it incorporates within its concern, and by the inherent lack of specificity of common-sense convergence of thought.

In the face of its limitations theology can only discredit itself if it claims more than it can produce. In this most comprehensive of human endeavors there exists the most serious need for a pervasive Christian humility.

THE LIMITS OF THEOLOGY

T HE contemporary challenge to theology, both from within and from the outside of the Christian community, is essentially the demand that it specify the means by which it proposes to reach conclusions and submit to the appropriate criticism the conclusions so drawn. If theology is to justify its claim to being a serious and significant human enterprise, it must be prepared to define its method of procedure and in so doing to indicate in what sense it contends that its conclusions are "true," "meaningful," or "reliable." There is no occasion for it to accept the criteria which are suggested from outside theology, but in lieu of this it must provide its own critical apparatus.

It is not incumbent on theology, any more than upon any other human enterprise, to present a system for which it is maintained that it contains all relevant truth. It is incumbent upon theology that its conclusions be derived in a manner consistent with the specified methodology and that they be able to bear the criticism of the system of determination which produces them. It need not expect that its conclusions will receive universal acceptance, but it can at least make plain the basis of their meaningfulness and the nature of their certitude. It may expect that its work will be subjected to criteria which it has not made explicitly a part of its procedure —pragmatic, aesthetic, or sentimental standards which have some bearing upon its appeal—and these may be anticipated as a matter of practical concern. In other words, theology *must* be faithful to its own specified method of procedure and *may* well seek to meet other standards for the sake of general acceptability.

Focusing as it does upon ultimate significance, theology must be able to formulate those conclusions which it finds convincing and must rely upon its method of derivation as the means by which those conclusions are certified. The manner in which A. N. Whitehead describes the task of theology is both realistic and challenging: "I do not hold it to be possible, or even desirable, that identity of detailed belief can be attained. But it is possible that amid diversities of belief, arising from differences of stress exhibited in metaphysical insight and from differences of sympathetic intuition respecting historical events,—that it is possible, amid these differences, to reach a general agreement as to those elements, in intimate human experience and in general history, which we select to exemplify that ultimate theme of the divine immanence, as a completion required by our cosmological outlook. . . . The task of Theology is to show how the World is founded on something beyond mere transient fact and how it issues in something beyond the perishing of occasions. The temporal World is the stage of finite accomplishment. We ask of Theology to express that element in perishing lives which is undying by reason of its expression of perfections proper to our finite natures."[1]

The essential method of theology is that of effecting a comprehensive and common-sense convergence of evidence of all orders of knowledge and insight as they bear upon the determination of ultimate meaning for man. In the discerning and recognition of contributory evidence it must take into consideration all appropriate logical and empirical derivations for which it can find relevance, and in so doing must operate by the same logical and empirical procedures which commend themselves for general acceptance; but it must also acknowledge as contributory the hairetic determinations which the more objective disciplines endeavor to ignore. The crucial test to which theology must submit itself in its convergence has its subjective pole, even as it has introduced subjective elements into its determinations. It aspires to create a state of certitude, the certitude which does not presuppose pure objective knowledge but expresses itself directly as the unqualified disposition to act. In this sense theology acknowledges a final practical criterion; its formulations are to be tested by their capacity to elicit unqualified commitment of self.

There are certain limits to the possible accomplishments of theology. It must aspire to nothing less than ultimate understanding and must undertake to incorporate all relevant truth of all orders, but it must also acknowledge its inescapable limitations. For theology to claim to have accomplished, or be in a position to accomplish, too much is to discredit what would otherwise be its valid conclusions. When the theologian has been unable or unwilling to recognize inherent limitations, when he has insisted that his formulations be taken as a final and authoritative expression of truth, he has simply invited that the whole structure be discarded upon the demonstration of the first significant flaw. He can in safety and honesty claim for his work only that degree of certitude which his method is competent to produce.

Theology must deal with the entire range of human concerns and attempt to determine their relevance for ultimate concern. Accordingly, the limitations which theology acknowledges do not refer to scope. Rather, they refer to the degree of possible success with which theology may presume to accomplish its task. This does not mean merely the limitations of some particular mind nor the incompleteness of tracing out all possible implications. It is the acknowledgment of certain methodological limitations which no degree of expansion can hope to overcome—a sort of "built-in" restriction. Because it undertakes to render intelligible truths which are, by definition, beyond complete appropriation, theology must be conscious of the fact that even its best expressions will be lacking in specificity. Because it seeks to present in objective form insights and responses which are highly subjective, its formulations must fall short of both theoretical and practical adequacy. Because of the incompleteness of subordinate knowledge, it cannot presume that its convergence of such knowledge is final or absolute.

A part of the methodological task of theology is that of indicating its inherent limitations, of vindicating its approach by claiming only that degree of certitude or formal validity which it is competent to produce. In so doing theology serves to delimit its claims to substantiate those affirmations which are appropriate to its approach to understanding.

The Limits Imposed by Language

Theology, like all other activities which undertake to exhibit understanding or express truth, is to a large degree dependent upon the language, written or spoken, which serves as its vehicle of communication. It can render its affirmations intelligible only to the degree that it can find words which will serve as adequate bearers of meaning. Theology has no means of moving beyond the potentialities of the linguistic forms of its communication.

There is no purpose to be served by engaging in a detailed discussion of the priority of language for thought or of thought for language. Whether there exist concepts, abstract or concrete, apart from a form of linguistic representation is a question which need not be settled. Even though we were to accept the view that there are certain religious truths for which there are no corresponding words or symbols, we would still be forced to recognize that theology is forced to communicate those concepts in some verbal fashion. Reichenbach's observations concerning the relationship between thought and language are as significant for theology as for any other human endeavor: "A rationally reconstructed knowledge can only be given in the language form—that needs no further explanation, since it may be taken as a part of the definition of what we call rational reconstruction. So we are entitled to limit ourselves to symbolized thinking, *i.e.*, to thinking formulated in language, when we begin with the analysis of knowledge. If anyone should raise the objection that we leave out by this procedure certain parts of thinking which do not appear in the language form, the objection would betray a misunderstanding of the task of epistemology; for thinking processes enter into knowledge, in our sense of the term, only in so far as they can be replaced by chains of linguistic expression. Language, therefore, is the natural form of knowledge."[2]

The point which Reichenbach makes is especially relevant for theology in the sense that the theological task is one of "reconstructive thinking." It is the task not only of searching for meaning but also of framing that meaning in some form which can be communicated with a minimum loss of mutual understanding.

Theology is not alone in encountering the difficulty of finding words appropriate to convey its meanings. Every form of inquiry which reaches beyond the most commonplace discourse concerning empirical data is faced with the problem of finding adequate linguistic representation. The effort may be made to use the elements of ordinary language by employing qualifying phrases to indicate the exact sense in which familiar words are appropriated. As an alternative, theology may turn to a "technical vocabulary," a language composed of archaic or coined terms, which is free from the undesired coloration of familiar terms but which must, at some point, be explained in familiar language if it is to be more than a cabalistic jargon.

Whatever device theology employs, it is still limited by the restrictions of the mode of representation it chooses. The use of language, technical or popular, limits theology to that meaning which language is able to convey. Theology may speak of empirical facts and logical relationships with neither more nor less precision than may philosophy or science. When it seeks to reach beyond the area of immediate awareness, it is still compelled to use words which have arisen within the context of sensory experience and which, perforce, must lose some degree of specificity in employing them in another context. The degree of correspondence between the symbol employed and the object or idea which is represented may vary widely, but theology cannot perform its task without calling into service words which are admittedly vague in reference. Cultural coloration and emotional overtones of crucial terms make it impossible to convey exact objective denotation. If we speak of God as "person," "loving," or "spirit," the words are inevitably colored by the conceptual framework of the writer and reader. If we use such terms as "lord," "father," or "judge," individual experience and sociological setting will determine in large measure the meaning which is conveyed; there will be an approximation of idea but not an identity of concept for any two individuals who use the terms. The words "sin," "faith," or "eternal" may be explained but not defined to a degree which will eliminate the differences of individual thought forms. The terms by which we explain them are, in

their turn, subject to the same ambiguity and personal coloration.

The most serious limitation upon theology imposed by the
necessary reliance upon language is the impossibility of con-
structing basic statements in such form that they are genuinely
propositional. If theology were to operate within the pattern
of strict deductive reasoning for all or any significant part of
its work, it would be necessary for it to be able to reduce its
general statements to propositional form. The language of
theology, however, does not permit this. Many, if not most,
of the basic terms of theology must be recognized as of the
nature of metaphors rather than rigorous formulation. Deductions, therefore, from such statements, propositional in
appearance but lacking logical definiteness, are of necessity
something less than clear inferences.

Theology has frequently encountered difficulty when it has
lost sight of the metaphorical nature of some of its utterances.
References to God in terms of sovereignty, fatherhood, or person all have their significance for theology, but as soon as
such references are treated as propositions and made the basis
for strict inference they lead into confusion and distortion.
Similarly, such terms as "adoption," "ingrafting," "redemption," and "regeneration," when their metaphorical force is
kept in mind, serve well to convey basic insights; but they
can easily result in serious aberration if they are assumed to
be examples of unequivocal communication.

Even though it be maintained that theological discourse
refers to concepts and insights which are not of "natural"
derivation, it can use only "natural" language. In so far as it
must appropriate such terminology and employ it in some
larger context it does so only by sacrificing some degree of
the specificity of the terms employed. We are dealing not with
identities but with analogies. Whether we prefer to think in

terms of the classical *analogia entis* or of the *analogia fidei* we are still in the position of employing language which has only approximate appropriateness. Discourse in analogy and argument from analogy bear the serious limitation of demanding that the terms employed be taken in some sense other than a complete one-to-one correspondence of the symbol and the reality symbolized. This form of discourse or argument has the power of suggesting meanings or insights of profound significance, but they do not provide the basis of a rigorous logical procedure.

Barth has focused attention upon the responsibility of theology for examining the language in which the Church speaks of God as the primary function of dogmatics.[3] In speaking from its experience the Church is often pressed to find any mode of communication which is even approximately satisfactory. The language of religion is characteristically rich in poetic expression, in metaphors borrowed from all areas of objective fact and subjective experience. If theology is to do full justice to this religious expression it cannot help but resort to many of the same poetic forms which permeate the life of the Christian community. In other words, in seeking to provide an intelligible formulation theology must employ language which at times has suggestive and poetic significance, rather than clear propositional character.

In performing its constructive and apologetic function there is no reason why theology should not so employ language. However, in its critical function it must be conscious of what is taking place. More specifically, it can extract from poetic utterances only that sort of certitude which they are designed to produce. Theology can quite properly attempt to suggest meanings beyond that of most unimaginative components of language, but when it does so it must not treat these poetic utterances as if they were logical propositions.[4]

A second limitation imposed by theology's dependence

upon language arises from the changing nature of language in time. The fact is too generally recognized to require belaboring that the gross and subtle modifications which take place within any living language are such that no theological formulation of one generation may be presumed to serve following generations. The contention that the truths conveyed are of unchanging nature is totally beside the point. The means by which they are conveyed change so significantly that the continuing critical function of theology is that of examining the adequacy of a theological construction not only in terms of the truths it proposes to present but also in terms of the thought forms of the individuals or groups to whom it is to be conveyed.

In brief, this is an inescapable limitation with reference to the finality or continuing adequacy of any theological construction. No formulation can serve beyond the point at which its linguistic elements have undergone significant modification. This is especially true with regard to those poetic elements which are incorporated within a theological construction. Even where the denotative force of a word remains constant, there are aesthetic and emotional overtones which can become modified to the extent that the word carries a force quite different from that which was originally intended.[5]

This changing force of language, particularly of poetic language, always poses a special problem for Biblical theology. In this area where an appeal is made to documents which are richly metaphorical and only occasionally systematic in form tremendous care must be exercised in an appeal to the normative character of a particular utterance. The same caution holds, however, for the whole body of theology. The normative significance of any form of discourse is limited to the extent that the original force can be preserved or recaptured.

In acknowledging the limits which language places upon

theology it is possible, of course, to overemphasize the restrictions of discourse. Theology, along with all other branches of inquiry, must rely upon the common-sense balance which is recognized between the two poles of the fact that, obviously, the communication involved in language is seldom complete, but that, equally obviously, some meaning is communicated.

The preoccupation with problems of semantics which has characterized much of twentieth-century thought is far from futile. We cannot escape the acknowledgment that while language—even when the greatest care is exercised in its use —is far from a perfect vehicle, it still remains our best vehicle. The work of theology is inexorably tied to the potentialities and limitations of language. It need not delude itself into supposing that its mode of expression is either formally perfect or temporally final. It must appeal in a greater degree than do some of the more limited inquiries to language which is metaphorical in character, for the sake of suggesting meanings which lie beyond explicit definition. This reliance upon the symbolic potentialities of language is no essential mark of weakness. It becomes a weakness only to the extent that this symbolic character is ignored or denied.

Susanne Langer and Philip Wheelwright,[6] among many others, have called attention to the damage that is done to all forms of inquiry when the effort is made to restrict language to its most unimaginative levels, or when the symbolic potentialities of language are obscured in misdirected aspiration for emotion-free communication. Theology need not fall into the snare of restricting itself to prosaic specificity, but it can resort to the broader resources of communication only by understanding and acknowledging what it is doing.

The witness of the Christian community includes many forms of communication other than verbal expression. The symbolic testimony of sacraments, the quality of life of individuals in the broader community, the visual presentation of architecture, all have significance in the total witness. To these things theology may point at times, but its function of intelligible and orderly presentation calls for an almost exclusive reliance upon the power of words. These words it may employ in both explicit and metaphorical force. It cannot, however, either define or suggest meanings which are not within the compass of language. Neither can it afford to forget the symbolic character of all language and the special restrictions which apply to the use of poetic expression.

The Limit Imposed by Subjective Reference in Theology

Two features of theological inquiry are reciprocally self-limiting. The systematic aim of its endeavor and the inclusion of subjective reference within its scope preclude the simultaneous accomplishment of the two aspirations. Systematization is possible only where there exists a complete objectification of the data. This, theology cannot presume to do without violating the essential feature of the human responses which it seeks to consider. Serious consideration of the elements of personal choice and individual response involved in theological determinations are of such nature that they cannot be sufficiently objectified for genuine systematization.

When theology undertakes to correlate all significant awareness, *including the subjective responses and choices of individuals,* for the sake of the determination of ultimate meaning, it is caught in the dilemma of having to sacrifice full systematization or to surrender the consideration of some part of its data. The objective description of the choices and responses involved are a real part of the theological task, but intelligible description requires a reduction to categories of thought. Every step taken in the direction of more precise objective description is a step away from the essential subjective character of the response which is being described.

The protest of the existentialists against oversystematization applies to theology more directly than to any other human concern. An inquiry of more restricted scope can well afford to construct an entirely coherent and plausible scheme, *even if it does so by deliberately and consciously excluding from its domain all subject matter which doesn't fit the scheme*. Structural consistency can always be purchased at the expense of comprehensiveness. Because of the impossibility of imposing on theology a limit in scope, it must be prepared to accept a limited success in systematic formulation.

This is not to say that theology is under no obligation to present its findings in as clear and logical a form as it can find. Forced to choose between a sacrifice of genuine coherence for the sake of inclusiveness and the surrender of certain aspects of reality for the sake of systematic formulation, the theologian has no warrant for making either the sole criterion. In the first instance he will find himself making assertions which exhibit no strict logical bond with others of his affirmations. In the second case he will find himself ignoring relevant and significant witness simply because he has no conceptual category in which it can be structured.

The Limits to Systematic Formulation Arising from the Acknowledgment of Uniqueness

Closely associated with the limit to systematization imposed by the incorporation of subjective reference is the limit arising from the positing of *uniqueness*. Theology must deal not only with the particular incidents of experience which may be classified according to more general orders but must also deal with the unique incident. (See pp. 68 ff.) To consider God among a general class of "spiritual beings" is to do violence to the central task of theology.[7] To deal with the Incarnation as if it were one instance of a more general class of divine effusions is to deny the central thing which theology would seek to assert about the Incarnation. To talk about an ultimate meaning of human existence is not to consider one meaning among others. That which is ultimate is also unique.

Once we make place for uniqueness we have precluded the possibility of genuine systematization. We may have some means of indicating or suggesting but not of defining the incident to which we refer. To find within the unique incident certain elements which it shares with particular members of certain recognized classes provides us with some intelligible contact. It does not enable us, however, to reduce the unique incident to systematic formulation.

The Limit Involved in the Method of Convergence

Theology must appeal to logical, experiential, authoritative, and hairetic determinations in its constructions and must employ the criteria of all of them for its meaning and verification. No one of these alone, however, can be accorded final jurisdiction in passing upon the others or in effecting a synthesis of them. The method of convergence in theology is that of a "common-sense" integration of them all, an effort to determine the particular areas in which specific appeals are appropriate and an endeavor to accord appropriate weight to the various forms of evidence.

As has already been acknowledged (see pp. 141 ff.), there are serious limitations to such a procedure. The necessity for "adding incommensurables" precludes the possibility of a precise conclusion. The general area of truth in which some convergence of evidence may appear is, even at best, a rather broad area. This is particularly true since theology has found it of significance to incorporate within its considerations certain observations which must be communicated through metaphorical language. No precise convergence can possibly result once non-precise elements have been introduced.

In order to describe the type of limit to which theological convergence is subject it is important to keep in mind the form of certitude which it endeavors to produce. Only within the confines of a purely formal logical system can the certitude of logical necessity appear, and only within a setting of empirical induction can the validation of sensory evidence be presented as final. The certitude which is the end product of theology is neither that of necessity nor of immediate experience but that of commitment.

Logic and experience function as negative requirements, setting up the range within which genuine choices may be made. Theology functions critically to specify as closely as possible the genuine alternatives concerning which choice may be exercised. It may point historically to certain choices which have been made, may call attention to the fact that some choice is necessary. It cannot, however, demonstrate that one choice or another is either logically necessary or empirically vindicated. To do so would, in fact, be a denial of the genuineness of the choice involved.

The convergence in theological method may be expected to produce only that form of certitude appropriate to it, the certitude which means that the individual is prepared to act with unqualified commitment of himself to the choice involved. Certain hypothetical possibilities may be demonstrated to be not genuine possibilities, self-contradicting or empirically invalidated. Within the range of those possibilities which are genuine, however, theology can only indicate that a commitment is open to the individual.

Meaning and Truth in Theology

The minimum claim of theology which justifies its place as a human inquiry is that of *meaningfulness*. The more demanding test is that of *truthfulness*. The two are, of course, interrelated. No formulation could contend that it is true unless it possessed meaning. On the other hand, the meaningfulness of a formulation is dependent upon the sense in which it purports to be true.

The meaningfulness of theological utterances, and of theological formulations as a whole, cannot be determined by a single standard of reference. Since theology draws into itself as a proper part of its concern those rational and empirical considerations which make up the body of science and philosophy, it employs in those areas the same contexts of meaning which are appropriate to the particular disciplines. In dealing, however, with those determinations which lie outside scientific and philosophical consideration—subjective response, unique event, hairetic determination—theology must find its meaning in terms of the commitment of the person. These determinations are meaningful in the sense that they describe the conceptual constructions which would form the basis of particular lines of conduct and decision. It is, thereby, *limited* to this standard of meaning; not that every element in theology is devoid of other meaning, but that its comprehensive contribution has a meaning of this order.

The question still remains in what sense theology can present its formulations to be *true*. Certainly it is important that theology not delude itself, nor seek to delude individuals, in presuming that its conclusions have the full force of logical necessity or of genuine empirical verification. These criteria may properly be applied to component elements of the theological undertaking, but they may not be presumed to furnish a basis on which the entire theological structure can be validated. Neither can theology, having included within its scope the subjective responses of individuals, take its stand upon the ground that it asserts *pure objective truth*.

The epistemological question and the ontological are inseparable. There can be no separation of *truth of what is* from *truth as known*. Truth apart from truth as prehended is an unjustified abstraction. Accordingly, there is no reason for theology to seek to avoid the fact that the truth it presents must be regarded, in part at least, as truth which has a strong psychological orientation. It is that description which finds assent, for whatever impulse, on the part of individuals or groups; that which meets the test of being adequate for the needs of an individual or community. This pragmatic test does not constitute the entire meaning of truth for theology, but it is a significant one.

Only by moving past this pragmatic reference can theology exercise its critical function. It must possess some standard other than, "It satisfies me," if it is to regard some theological constructions as false or true, sound or unsound. In the final analysis, the test which theology must apply is that of asking whether the choices which are presented are genuine choices. A sound theology is one which presents clearly the nature of the determinations which ultimately must be resolved in terms of decision. A "false" theology is one which distorts or obscures the nature of the choices involved.

There are several ways in which a theological construction may serve to cloud rather than clarify the choices involved in life. It is possible on the one hand to present as matters of choice—as articles of faith—determinations which are subject to empirical or logical determination. It is possible on the other hand to obscure the fact that certain determinations rest upon decisions of the individual, to create the delusion that the decisions are reached by logical process or by inferential knowledge.

The work of theology is, in this sense, limited to a defining of those areas in which choice is unavoidable, to marking out as clearly as possible the nature of the alternatives which exist. It may employ logical and empirical criteria to indicate those apparent decisions which leave no real alternatives. It cannot, however, eliminate choice from human determinations and must seek, therefore, to present these choices as essential components of knowledge and understanding.

The limit of objective truth in theology is the degree to which it can specify the areas and nature of choices which present themselves. It cannot objectively determine which choice *must* be made. It can, as it speaks from within the Church and shares the witness of the Church, indicate what decisions have been made by an historic community. To do so is not to claim that it has presented an objectively vindicated determination but one which is objectively limited and demanding of some type of decision not made for the subject either by logical necessity or empirical evidence.

The Necessity for Humility in Theology

Although humility has been presented traditionally as the crowning grace of Christian virtue, Christian theology has not consistently exemplified that redeeming quality. It is understandable that in religion's demand for a full commitment of life there should be a call for a positive affirmation which avoids all uncertainties and all spirit of tentativeness.

Skepticism, suspended judgment, qualified assent, would seem to belong to the realm of science and philosophy rather than to the realm of theology. It is in its desire to avoid this seeming display of weakness or indecision that theology can easily make its position most vulnerable. "The more perfect the dogmatism, the more insecure. A great high topsail that can never be reefed nor furled is the first carried away by the gale."[8] It is reluctance on the part of theology to acknowledge the limits of its own accomplishments and to restrict the claims of its finality which results in excessive pretentions of its adherents. It is these excessive pretentions which make it vulnerable and which invite a general discrediting of its work.

Nowhere is Cromwell's plea more pertinent than when directed to theology "to consider the possibility that it might be wrong." Regarding the objective components of its formulations, theology is under the same limitation that invests all forms of inquiry, the confines of experience and of rational analysis. With reference to the subjective responses which theology must consider it cannot even describe them with unequivocal precision, certainly cannot present its descriptions as final or normative. It must deal with the question of what is ultimate for man but cannot suppose that the form of its answer is ultimate. It rests for its meaning upon a commitment which is unqualified but it cannot claim that unqualified assent to the formulations which it produces.

In the course of its work theology must call attention to the corrupting effect of egocentricity upon all levels of human reason, and in doing so must bring itself under the same judgment. The pride of the autonomous intellect may be strengthened rather than overcome by the appeal to the revelatory reference which is essential to theology. John Dewey's warning is not without force and historic justification: "The pride of the zealously devout is the most dangerous form of pride. There is a divisive pride of the learned, as well as of family wealth and power. The pride of those who feel themselves learned in the express and explicit will of God is the most exclusive. Those who have this pride, one that generates an exclusive institutionalism and then feeds and sustains itself through its connection with an institution claiming spiritual monopoly, feel themselves to be special organs of the divine, and in its name claim authority over others. . . . The sense of dependence that is bred by recognition that the intent and effort of men are never final but are subject to the uncertainties of an indeterminate future, would render dependence universal and shared by all. It would terminate the most corroding form of spiritual pride and isolation, that which divides man from man at the foundation of life's activities. A sense of common participation in the inevitable uncertainties of existence would be coeval with a sense of common effort and shared destiny."[9]

The honesty which is incumbent upon theology and the humility which is becoming to it alike call for a frank recognition of that which its methodology is competent to produce. Theology can speak intelligibly of that which transcends nature as well as of that which lies within nature, but in order to do so it must appeal to forms of discourse which are metaphorical in construction and limited in their logical precision. It can strive for a high measure of consistency but cannot force within the standards of reason those conclusions which it confesses to rest upon non-rational derivations. It can relate the transcendent considerations which are its primary concern to those immediate and penultimate considerations drawn from ordinary thought and experience, but it cannot employ its transcendent insights as generalizations from which it can prescribe standards to which experience must conform. It can effect an integration by virtue of its broader scope which is not possible for more restricted disciplines, but the convergence by which this integration is effected produces a field in which decision is to be made, rather than a ready-made decision.

For the sake of intelligibility theology seeks to reduce to some systematic expression all the witness of the Christian community, as well as the universal elements of human experience. It cannot, however, find firm categories which make complete systematization possible. The uniqueness of divine initiative and the uniqueness of each human response do not submit themselves to the sort of objectification which definitive systems require. The systems which theology constructs are a product of a significant human enterprise, but they are always something less than the subject matter with which they deal. Measured in terms of their adequacy for communication between men, and in terms of their success in generalizing the community of belief from which they spring, these systems may stand among the more important accomplishments of man. Measured, however, against the subject matter with which they have aspired to deal, they must be viewed as "broken lights" of the reality they endeavor to reflect.

The successful pursuit of the theological enterprise calls for the suggesting of meanings which cannot be precisely specified. In this sense theology becomes a work involving artistic creation and criticism. Religious knowledge must be presented in some symbolic form. It is theology's task to devise and examine the means of such symbolic communication.

A large part of the truth with which theology must deal is non-propositional in character. This form of truth must be suggested by poetic constructions rather than reduced to objectively verifiable propositions. Theology is not less than a science but more than a science. It is closely akin to all those forms of artistic creation and criticism which seek to suggest meanings transcending those of precisely specified reference.

THE SYMBOLIC PRESENTATION
OF NON-PROPOSITIONAL TRUTH

THE limits to which theology is subject are such that it cannot anticipate a genuine accomplishment of its aspiration. Because of its subjective content and non-empirical reference, because of its frank endeavor to speak concerning an ultimate meaning which is asserted to be neither experientially nor rationally derived, theology cannot suppose that it will be able to present its truths in a form which has the internal coherence of a mathematical system or the sensory validation of a scientific hypothesis. Nonetheless, theology is still engaged in the task of presenting that which it wishes to have recognized as "true," in bringing that truth within a formulation which is genuinely intelligible if not rigorously logical, in commending its conclusions as interpretable in terms of human experience and response even if not derived from such experience.

The Symbolic Element in Religious
Communication

The successful exercise of the theological enterprise rests upon the honest appropriation of a fact which is usually freely recognized for religion in general but is seldom acknowledged regarding theology specifically. This is the fact of dependence upon symbolic representation as a primary vehicle of meaning for religious discourse. In the whole range of religious expression visual, verbal, and ritualistic symbols occupy an essential place. These symbols are designed to stimulate the imagination, to create a mood or attitude, to suggest a direction of contemplation rather than to describe a specific concept or element of experience. In no case are these symbolic presentations deemed to be identical with the reality which they are intended to suggest.

The Biblical, traditional, sacramental heritage of the Christion community is one which is incomprehensible apart from this symbolic presentation. Even the creeds of the Church are quite properly designated "creedal symbols." The Biblical exegete has as his primary task the function of grasping the metaphorical import of his material and selecting that set of symbols which will speak to one age with the force which was originally conveyed through the suggestive figures of speech of an earlier generation. The traditional formulations of the Church—creeds, confessions, ecclesiastical pronouncements, ritualistic practices—are all creative efforts to find appropriate *symbols* for truths for which there are no definite *signs*.[1] This is most strikingly obvious with reference to the sacraments of the Church. When the question is raised, "What do these sacraments mean?" it is relevant to seek to convey in language some approximation of the same meaning. In part, however, the answer must always be, "If the meaning were expressible in words, then the Church would have long ago dispensed with the symbolic act."

It is not a matter of chance or perversity which accounts for the prevalence of myth, parable, poetry, and art as the dominant media of religious communication. Rather, it is a manifestation of the fact that meanings must be suggested which cannot be precisely described. Poetry, in its proper sense, is the natural language of religion. It is a conscious creation, a reliance upon imaginative representation and imaginative response to convey the primary meaning of discourse.

Poetry, of course, is not primarily a matter of rhyme and meter. It is figurative or symbolic communication, and its distinctive reliance is upon *metaphor* as a basic communicative device.[2] Quite a number of figures of speech may be classified by the literary critic, but the metaphor is clearly recognizable as the most general of these and as the one to which all others may be reduced. In this sense, the myth and parable are expanded or extended metaphors. The power of all such poetic devices lies in the fact that more meaning can be suggested than is specifically defined. The very essence of the metaphor is that its elements are *not identities*.

Undisguised metaphor runs throughout Scriptural literary form. Israel is to be seen as a family, a flock of sheep, a child, a harlot, a mass of clay in the potter's hands. Jehovah is a king, a man of war, a husband, a father, a shepherd. Nowhere could be found richer imagery than that used with reference to Jesus Christ, both in His own references and in the poetic creations of the early Church. He is a door, a vine, the bread from heaven, a lamb, a star, a rose, the cornerstone of a building. The Church is a body, an army, the new holy nation, a lamp, yeast, salt, a priestly order. In each, the poetic imagery suggests undefined similarities, stimulates the prehension of a meaning which is lost when literal identification is presumed.

The expanded metaphor which takes the form of myth or parable is even more prominent in the Scriptural form of communication. Some of these are so frankly symbolic in nature that there is no real danger of misunderstanding. The preaching of the prophets from Nathan to Jonah abounds with stories in which the literal meaning is completely subordinated to the figurative. The parables of Jesus, though sometimes subjected to literalistic distortion, are so clearly metaphorical in character that any effort to look upon them in any light other than the poetic must produce ludicrous results.[3] Not infrequently, "bad" theology is the direct product of ascribing literalistic meanings to parabolic teaching.

There can be no avoiding the realization that in Scripture there are sections in which the form of communication is neither clearly figurative nor purely literal. Rather, as in many other literary forms, there are passages in which the two forms of communication are interwoven or indistinct. Interestingly enough, the major divisions of exegetical work and patterns of interpretation are not over the question of whether or not "the Bible is to be interpreted literally." Rather, the question is *which* passages are to be taken literally and *which* figuratively.[4] Very diverse notions as to "what the Bible really teaches" can be derived by simply appealing to literal meaning in those passages which one finds supporting his own viewpoint and by ascribing symbolic meanings to those passages which would be difficult or contradictory if taken literally.

The patristic and medieval pattern of seeking to find in every section of Scripture not a single form of teaching but multiple meanings was a reflection of the persisting awareness that literal meaning alone does violence to Biblical thought forms. The insistence upon finding moral and spiritual allegories as well as literal meaning in every passage of Scripture produced many religious oddities. Distortions can arise from imposing symbolic overtones to literal communication as well as from ignoring figurative coloration. The insistence upon multiple meanings which characterized exegesis for centuries was misdirected in the sense that it refused to acknowledge that there can be in the sacred writings a form of communication which is as literal and straightforward as a cookbook or an encyclopedia. It did, however, exhibit a sensitivity to the basic spirit of symbolic communication with which the Scriptures abound.

Present trends in Biblical interpretation reflect a willingness to retain this sensitivity to symbolic overtones without forcing allegorical meanings upon the entire Biblical record. A major contribution to Christian thought is made by Rudolf Bultmann and the many others who have shared his efforts in seeking to catch the symbolic overtones of Biblical thought and transmit them by a type of symbolic transformation. In this form of Biblical study there can be no wooden reliance upon a single formula. Instead there must be a knowledge and appreciation of the prevailing thought forms in which the message is communicated, and a readiness to respond to those conscious or unconscious metaphors to which a writer appeals.

The continuing witness of the Church has not been a program of reducing or removing the symbolic element in religious communication. On the contrary, the number and variety of symbolic presentations has grown with the passing years. Each social unit which has received the Christian message in a form determined by its traditions exercises some degree of invention and imagination in appropriating from its own experience certain familiar elements which can be used as metaphoric expression of the religious truth it has received. The hymnody, sermonic proclamation, and personal witness of the Church have tended to preserve the traditional symbolism through which it has received the message, while modifying and enriching it through the introduction of newly appropriated vehicles of thought.[5]

The Essential Place of Symbolic Expression in Theology

The prevailing common-sense notion that theology is distinguished by its systematic and intellectualized formulation is well founded. There is a real sense in which theology, as distinct from devotional or lyrical expressions of religion, is an endeavor to make a more precise presentation of Christian truth than is possible through aesthetic or emotional appeals. In fact, there is a certain validity in the assumption that it is just here that theology is not co-terminal with religion, i.e., that the task of theology is that of reducing to lucid and literal language the essential truths which are witnessed to by the liturgy, sacraments, and proclamation of the Church as it employs symbolism as a means of communication. Quite properly the Church and the secular world assume that the theologian is to present his work in a form which places a premium upon cognitive meaning rather than upon aesthetic response.

There is no reason to obscure this distinctive feature of theology. However, because of the subject matter which it must treat theology may only alter or modify, not eliminate, the symbolic character of its discourse. It has no way of capturing within the limits of precise and unambiguous language insights which are themselves non-literal. It captures what it can, but always with the awareness that more has escaped through the meshes of the net than has been confined by the net. If it is to endeavor to present any approximation of the comprehensive concern of religion, it must say more than literal language can convey. In short, it must employ language with metaphoric force.

One experiences no difficulty in sensing that to speak of Jesus as "the Lamb of God" or "the Door to the sheepfold" is to call upon metaphoric expression. The theologian is called upon to "explain" the symbols, i.e., to make plain what these symbols suggest. However, if he is really to *make them plain* he is not engaged in replacing symbolic language by literal language (although he may do this in part), but in finding the symbols which will best convey to another person the meanings which have been suggested by the original metaphor.

The theologian does not operate without metaphor but by seeking to find metaphors which will serve to raise the level of cognitive content. Theology may find such expressions as "The Rose of Sharon" or "the Bright and Morning Star" aesthetically appealing but lacking in cognitive content. It may employ instead the expression "the manifestation of the glory of God." In doing so it has changed the context of symbolic reference rather than eliminated it.

The systematic requirement which rests upon theology calls for a higher degree of consistency in the use of symbols than is necessary for the lyrical or devotional expressions of religious insight. Because of the need for a cognitive content which is relatively higher than aesthetic content (a situation which may well be reversed in lyrical or devotional expressions), theology must choose a set of symbols whose dominant connotations are kept intact throughout the discourse. (When a group of worshipers are expressing their faith in song, there is no sensed incongruity in singing "A Mighty Fortress Is Our God" and immediately changing the metaphor in order to sing "The King of Love My Shepherd Is." Theology does not dispense with this mode of communication but must, for the sake of orderly thought, hold to a more nearly uniform mode of representation.) Theology, whether or not it be specifically designated *systematic theology,* is characterized by reliance upon symbols whose connotation may be maintained with minimum ambiguity.

Every major effort at the communication of truth seems to have the tendency to find in some area of experience the *basic* metaphors which best serve its ends. Various metaphysical systems have found in the fields of mechanics, biology, mathematics, or astronomy certain elements which serve as "root metaphors." Similarly, the philosopher of history seems to a degree dependent upon the figures of speech he can derive from our experience of the human individual, the cosmos, or some mechanical order. In the realm of theology there is a marked tendency to find in the interpersonal experiences of ordinary life the metaphors in which religious insight may best be couched. "Father," "Sovereign," "Judge," are alike derived from social experience; and although theology has at times treated them as if they were literal in reference, forgetting their symbolic quality and drawing from them quite precise inferences, it has thereby not enhanced their significance but rather detracted from their force.[6] Although it would be rather impractical to persist in the custom, there might be real value in consistently placing such words within quotation marks for the purpose of preserving the metaphoric force.

The functional terms of theology are likewise drawn freely from interpersonal analogy. "Redemption" and "atonement," "adoption" and "forgiveness," point to similarities rather than to identities. To recognize their poetic force is to say nothing one way or the other about the existence of "realities" which they are designed to suggest. It is simply to keep in focus the fact that metaphoric reference constitutes a basic mode of communication.

The metaphors of theology are not altogether interpersonal in reference, of course. To speak of heaven is to point to the vault of the sky and say, "But of course I don't really mean the sky." To select the phrase "Abraham's bosom" is more obviously metaphoric but is not essentially different as a form of discourse.

One way of pointing to the essential place of symbolic representation in theology is by focusing attention upon the manner in which poetic representations change in their force and call for revisions on the part of theology. The Fish as a symbol of Christ served only so long as the Christian world was a Greek-speaking world. The symbol of the Pelican, quite meaningful to the medieval world, would have meant nothing to the first century Church and means little more to the twentieth century. Even such basic symbols as "Father" or "family" undergo modification of force as a society changes from patriarchal to national in structure; a change which sometimes calls upon the theologian to suggest, "In order to preserve the symbol it may be necessary for us to keep in mind *a particular kind of father.*" Similarly, the metaphors based upon cosmologies and psychologies of a different age call for a reduction to different symbols, or at least for some verbal interpretation.

In emphasizing the place of metaphoric language in theology it is not intended to imply that all theological discourse is poetic or that no literal reference finds a place in theology. On the contrary, a large part of the subject matter of theology is such that its reference can be quite literal. This is inherent in the comprehensive scope of theology. Since it incorporates within its interest and concern the whole range of empirical data and objective inquiry as they may be related to the matter of man's ultimate concern, any subject may be drawn into theological considerations and treated with strict literal reference. Leaving aside for the moment the semantic awareness that all language is in some degree symbolic, we may assert that in those areas where theology shares a concern with science and philosophy, in the historical and empirical elements of its considerations, it employs language in the same literal fashion as do the other disciplines. There is no occasion for theology to "wax poetic" in discussing the cosmological, historical, and ethical considerations which it must incorporate. However, it must pass beyond this rather literal form of discourse.

Theology is not alone in employing figures of speech as necessary modes of communication. Plato must turn to the "myth" in order to suggest meanings which defy literal linguistic definition. Science must appeal to symbolic representations, whether in the form of models or formulae, which must be viewed as *suggesting* rather than *describing* the nature of things. This point need not be pressed to the degree of scorning efforts at literal representation in theology, philosophy, or science. In each there are levels of literal discourse, but in none of them can a complete literalism prevail.

Although other disciplines share in theology's need to employ symbolic, non-literal modes of communication, it is not surprising that for theology the need is to a degree more dominant. This arises from the fact that theology has frankly drawn subjective responses into the realm of its considerations, *and subjective responses can be represented only through symbolism.* Happiness, fear, guilt, confidence can never be described through ostensive definition. The external expressions associated with them are of the nature of *symbols* rather than *signs.* Certainly no manifestation of these responses serves to tell us what they are. Their presence may be indicated by some physical act, but all verbal descriptions must remain in the order of suggestion rather than literal description. Since theological discourse involves a full and frank reliance upon human responses, upon relational and subjective appropriations, the work of theology cannot be done apart from literal employment of symbolic representation which is poetic in character.

Fusion of Literal and Symbolic Representation

Within theological discourse the fusion of literal and symbolic communication is such that any effort to draw sharp lines of differentiation is futile. When the person of

Jesus is considered, literal elements are present and afford a basis for intelligible discussion, but these elements do not exhaust the meanings which theology must attempt to communicate. Even to employ the expanded term "Jesus Christ" is to introduce at least an element of subjective, responsive reference. Tillich's language in frequently writing of "Jesus, seen and understood as the Christ by the church" calls attention to this responsive element. To speak of "the Christ" is to call into reference the messianic anticipations of Judaism and the interpretative response of the entire Christian tradition. An objective component is present, but the coloration of the term is primarily subjective.

One way of pointing to the type of presentation involved is through focusing attention upon similar descriptions in another area. If one is asked, "Who was Horatio Nelson?" and he responds, "A British admiral who lived from 1758 until 1805," he has chosen language which is dominantly literal in tone. If, however, he chooses the more interesting and informative response, "Nelson was the hero of Trafalgar," a highly subjective and valuational element has been injected into what is in form a statement of fact. The information which is being conveyed is, "Nelson is the man who, *as he is viewed and understood by English-speaking people,* is greatly to be admired in terms of his role in the battle of Trafalgar." The word "hero" is of such nature that it takes on meaning only within the context of evaluative response. It tells us something only by virtue of a response of admiration characteristic of some person or group of persons. Similarly, to assert that Jesus was a Galilean teacher who lived during three specific decades of the Roman Empire is to make a statement in which the objective content is dominant and is subject to standard historical verification. To make the more informative and interesting assertion that He is "the Christ," "the

Messiah," or "the Son of God," is to introduce elements which are valuational and consequently dependent upon subjective reference.

Many of the characteristic terms of theology are of this order; they do contain objectively referential elements, but they draw most of their significance from subjective reference. If the assertions be made: "God is (or is not) personal," "The Holy Spirit still speaks to men today," "Jesus Christ is the Redeemer of all mankind"; an effort, and a significant one, is being made *to say something about transcendent reality*. It is possible to do so, however, only by drawing freely upon symbolically presented subjective response as a context of exposition. We are, in effect, endeavoring to say something *about transcendent reality* through the means of saying something *about characteristic human responses*.

When we expand these affirmations, the subjective component becomes quite clear. The bare assertion, "God is personal," might be expanded thus: "God" is not a synonym for "person," and He may not be presumed to be defined by equating His nature with the form of being which we experience in interhuman contacts. However, the manner in which we *respond* to Him—that is, in terms of a sense of obligation, confidence, devotion, or gratitude—is closely akin to the manner in which we respond to personal entities, certainly *more* closely akin to this manner of response than it is to the characteristic response we make to physical objects, abstract concepts, or imaginary products of our daydreams.

Similarly, when we assert that "the Holy Spirit speaks to men," we are not saying, "He makes audible, vocal sounds with His mouth which impinge upon the physical senses of men, and thereby transmits to them certain directions, information, or interpretation." A closer approximation of our intent is: "The Holy Spirit acts in such a manner that it is possible for human beings to *respond* to His actions *in a manner similar* to the response which is accorded to the human act of speaking." Here again, any effort to abstract some purely objective entity from the response involved is to lose sight of the type of communication which is desired, the communication of meaning in terms of characteristic response.

For the third example chosen, to assert that Jesus Christ is the Redeemer of all mankind is to say something about reality by saying something about human responses, actual and potential. We are asserting that His meaning must be defined by reference to the "sense of being redeemed" which is a part of the awareness of certain individuals, and which might well enter into the consciousness of any or all individuals.

In each of these cases mentioned—and the examples could be extended—there is no constructed or implied negative judgment regarding the reliability of the response which serves as a reference. Here is but an example of the inseparability of ontological and epistemological questions, a situation pervasive in all considerations of truth and meaning but brought to sharp focus in theological inquiry. Subjectivity, never completely absent from human judgments, is simply here recognized as an essential point of linguistic reference.

If we keep in mind this frank subjective reference, we are recognizing that formal theology, differing only in degree from the most lyrical expressions of religion, relies upon the description of human responses as a means of pointing to the realities with which it must deal. Further, if we keep in mind the fact that such responses can be represented only through symbols, we catch the sense in which theology must call upon metaphorical language as a primary vehicle of communication. It appeals to a revelation which is *received*, but the manner in which it is received must be described in non-literal terms. To indicate the fashion of prehension one may use the words "see," "hear," or "feel," but this is a borrowing of the analogy of sensory experience rather than a reference to a particular visual, auditory, or tactile sensation. Because these terms convey the idea of direct awareness, they serve reasonably well to suggest a meaning which may be grasped. Their employment, however, calls for some exercise of imagination, both in the selection and in the grasp of the symbols employed.

The Non-propositional Character of Revealed Truth

So long as the discourse of theology is confined to a description of events or entities which may be ostensibly designated, it can employ a propositional mode of communication. It can construct the same sort of generalized formulations based on experience which constitute the major part of literal discourse. More specifically, when it is making statements regarding historical events or describing the external qualities of human behavior, it may make its affirmations in a form which are in the strictest sense propositional and which are subject to the operational requirements of logical procedure. So long as reasonable care is exercised in preserving the clear and unequivocal reference of the terms involved, theology operates with no special limitations and with no special privileges. Statements regarding empirical facts, or regarding the implication from those facts, constitute an important part of theological discourse. Whenever they appear they are presented with exactly the same claim for acceptance which is appropriate in any other field of inquiry.

However, when theology undertakes to make statements or draw conclusions regarding transcendent reality or to speak in terms of ultimate meaning, when it seeks to communicate truth which is revealed rather than discovered, then it must move into a different level of discourse. At this point theology tends to preserve the propositional *form* of communication, but its statements are not, and cannot be, strictly propositional in character.

In order to avoid confusion it is important to make some distinction between the terms "sentence," "statement," and "proposition." Quite obviously it is possible to form sentences which are not statements; they may be questions, exclamations, or exhortations. This distinction need not be pressed. Just as a statement is a special type of sentence so a proposition is a special type of statement. Although there is not complete agreement even among logicians as to exactly what constitutes a proposition, it is possible to indicate the sense in which it is here employed. Basically a proposition is a statement of such order that it may serve as an element in rigorously logical thought. In order to meet this function it it would seem that it must meet the following minimum demands:

1. It must be a statement (or reducible to the form of a statement).
2. All significant elements in it must have clear and unambiguous reference.
3. It must be either true or false.
4. There must be some manner in which the statement itself, its antecedents, or its implications can be subjected to empirical or logical vindication.

The first and second of these requirements call for no special examination. The third, that a proposition must be either true or false, has some consequence for theological procedure.[7] Its importance comes into focus when we consider it along with the fourth requirement that there be *some* means of validating *either* the statement itself *or* some element in the logical chain of which it is a part. A statement may well be a proposition, i.e., either true or false, even though there is no possible way of checking the truth or falsity of the statement itself. (For instance, "Electrons move in regular orbits around the nucleus of an atom" or "The original manuscript of the Gospel of Mark was written in Greek" are both statements whose truth cannot be checked *directly*. Implications from the statements, however, can be checked.) However, if a statement itself is not subject to verification, and if it is not derived from some proposition whose truth may be determined, and if it can produce no inferences which may be checked, then it presents an isolated concept which is devoid of truth function.

Although a large number of statements which embody religious truth are propositional in character and make up a significant part of theological discourse, there are other statements which do not fall into this category. However, to assert that a proposition must be true or false is not to assert the converse that truth may be presented only in propositional form. There are other modes of discourse which can communicate truth. For instance, "George Washington was the father of his country" is a statement which serves to communicate a truth, even though its metaphorical tone makes its status as a proposition questionable.

In denying the propriety of regarding certain theological utterances as propositional there is no suggestion that they are thereby disqualified as bearers of truth. The reluctance which is sometimes encountered in religious circles to recognize this difference would seem to arise from the assumption that any meaning *different* from literal meaning is something *less* than literal meaning. This assumption finds its expression in such questions as: "Do you suggest that theology is *merely* poetry?" or "Can we content ourselves with the employment of theological language which is *merely* figurative language?" These questions exhibit the general notion that because literal statements can be simply verified or refuted they constitute a *superior* means of communication.

The issue is not one of superiority but of standards of different order. Dostoevsky's "fable" of the Grand Inquisitor transmits truth in a fashion appropriate to its subject matter, and its truth is neither superior nor inferior to Hooke's Law. The behavior of weights and springs can best be described through mathematical generalizations. An insight into the nature of freedom can best be communicated through poetic imagery.

The insistence upon the non-propositional character of the Christian Revelation which has come from a number of Biblical theologians is not an effort to relegate the Scriptures to some lower level of significance. It is rather an effort to focus attention upon the fact that, although the language of Scripture contains some statements which are propositional in character and others which may be propositional in form but not in character, revelation is not to be equated with any set of formal logical elements. It is possible to impart truth, to impart information if you will, which is not restricted to propositional expression.

A recognition that theology is called upon to employ non-literal or metaphorical exposition is not an indictment of its significance but a summons to creative activity. Art is not less than science. There may be some justification for contending that it is more than science, but it is more appropriate to recognize the difference without insisting upon any essential superiority. Theology possesses features of both science and art; science in the sense that it must take into consideration those features of experience which refer to sense data, art in the sense that it must discover or create symbolic representations of certain insights which are not directly bound up with empirical entities.

One characteristic of symbolic representation is that its proper field of function is in those areas in which ostensive definition is not operative. It is quite true that I may have a symbol—a word, for instance—which represents some concrete entity. If that entity is a present element of my immediate sense experience, the word which symbolizes it may still be useful, but it is not essential. As long as it is possible to bring to sensory awareness the entity in question, the symbol for it *may* be dispensed with.[8] At a different level of cognition, however, symbol is not a convenience but a necessity. When the symbol may not be referred directly to some entity represented, the only means of interpreting it is through the use of some related symbol. In no case is the symbol *identical* with the thing symbolized. The process of discourse is the employment of one metaphor to expand or enrich another metaphor.

The introduction of metaphorical reference precludes the possibility of treating the utterance which contains it as one would treat strict propositions. The logical inference from a proposition must be regarded as having the same truth value as that of the original proposition; quite properly, we describe the inference as "contained within it." This same condition does not hold for a statement which involves metaphorical reference. If I say, "God is my Father," the truth thereby suggested does not warrant my concluding that the color of my eyes is determined by the arrangement of certain genes which are a part of His being. The fact is that having used the word "father" metaphorically, I preclude the possibility of treating the statement which contains the word as if it were a logical proposition.

One of the most obvious metaphorical devices of theology, ancient and modern, is the appeal to knowledge by analogy. "Things not seen" are grasped and comprehended in terms of "things which do appear." The analogy is but one distinctive form of metaphor. It is but a way of saying, "like, but not exactly like." Whether we are dealing with Thomas Aquinas' *analogia entis* or the *analogia fidei* of Barth we are asserting that there are significant elements of comparison with the divine nature to be found either in the world of sensed being or in the realm of responsive faith. The problem of application of this principle arises from the fact that when we say, "but not exactly like," we have no quantitive measure of similarity. There is no basic reason why divine reality is not to be prehended in terms of analogy to the world of public fact or the world of subjective experience; in fact, it is impossible to imagine any other terms in which it may be prehended. However, analogy provides a mode of strict inference only in those instances where the degree of similarity may be precisely specified.[9] Analogy apart from quantitive specification of manner and degree of difference can serve well to suggest concepts or insights but not to draw literal conclusions.

If theology is to reach beyond the confines of immediate and empirical awareness it must employ some form of symbolic representation. The symbols must be drawn from the empirical realm but employed in a manner designed to suggest meanings which lie beyond that realm. What seems to be denied to theology in terms of specificity of meaning by the frank recognition of the metaphorical references employed is more than counterbalanced by the potentialities which can be realized. The paradox need not be a scandal and an offense to the theologian who recognizes the symbolic character of the terms which he employs. We do not charge the poet with inconsistency when he tells us that the eyes of his beloved are stars and, in the next breath, that they are pools of water. (We may, of course, charge him with literary fault if his metaphors become too mixed. This, however, is something quite different from charging him with error.) Similarly, the theologian employs expressions whose inferences must lead to confusion if taken literally. Treated as propositions they do not even merit the euphemism of "paradox" but should be designated bald contradiction.

The theologian may choose to employ both the words "Priest" and "King" as descriptive of the role of the Master. If he is not conscious of the metaphorical significance of his words, he may feel called upon to produce both Davidic and Levitic genealogies for these two hereditary offices. The questions of divine sovereignty and of human freedom, of the two natures of Christ, of the unity and trinity of the Godhead, involve linguistic paradox at any level of discourse, but these questions lead to inescapable contradiction if their expressions are treated as propositions.

Many, if not all, of the most acrimonious controversies of the Church have turned more upon the question of the adequacy of one set of symbols in preference to another rather than upon the truth which such symbols are selected to exhibit. The unitary and dual procession of the Spirit is not primarily a disagreement regarding facts but a disagreement regarding the manner in which the facts are to be symbolized. The same thing may be said regarding the "same or like substance" of the Father and the Son. Greek metaphysics, in which the concept of "substance" is a primitive term, provides a set of metaphors in which the Godhead may be discussed. The controversy raged over the manner in which these metaphors could be used.

In contending that much theological controversy has been at the level of disagreement over forms of symbolic representation rather than over facts, we are not suggesting that all such discussion is futile. On the contrary, a primary function of dogmatics is, as Barth contends, that of examining critically the language in which the Church speaks about God.[10] To say that we speak in symbols is not to say that one symbol is as good as another. For instance, with sensitive insight the Church has rejected the symbols of sexual generation and of metaphysical emanation as inappropriate symbols in which the relationship between God and the physical universe may best be described. Likewise, it has rejected illusion as a metaphor to describe the force of evil. Some symbolic representations are more apt than others. The function of theology is not that of freeing itself from the use of symbols but of determining the most adequate mode of expression. It is, as Whitehead has suggested, the task of expressing in terms proper to our finite lives that element which is undying by reason of its expressions of perfection.[11]

Good and Bad Theology

It is entirely proper to look upon certain formulations as being "good" theology, others "bad." Any theology which ignores the difference between literal and figurative communication, which mistakes its symbolic representations with the thing represented, is "bad" in the sense that it has needlessly exposed itself to the contradictions and confusion which arise from attempting to draw precise conclusions from ambiguous postulates. We may also produce bad theology by taking upon ourselves the task of defending, at all costs, a particular mode of symbolic representation to which we cling without considering whether or not those particular representations serve effectively to elicit any real conceptual response. By contrast, "good" theology must deal with symbols, primarily linguistic ones, but employ them with a conscious awareness that their power lies in what they can suggest rather than in what they can specify.

The ideal of theology is neither the syllogism nor the hymn. Both literal and poetic communication have their place. Rigorous logical procedure is both applicable and helpful at all those points where the entities or concepts involved can be designated in definite and unequivocal terms. In all such discussions theology functions under no special limitations and with no special privilege. It has no power, however, to reach beyond itself to any meanings other than those contained within its definitions and observations. The creative exercise of poetic imagination is essential in the communication of any truth which is not directly tied to immediate sensory experience. The hymn has served as a vehicle through which the theology of the Church has perpetuated and extended its message. It cannot afford, however, to dispense with the discipline that is afforded by the critique of logical examination.

For theology to look upon itself as the Queen of the Sciences is not an act of usurpation but of abdication. (Need it be said that we speak here not literally but in metaphor?) The task of theology is not that of reigning over the various efforts to draw generalized conclusions about the objective world. She participates in the activity but holds no favored place in the enterprise. Her work is more than that of science alone, for she must assume the role of artist, the creator of poetic representation through which meanings closed to objective inquiry can be suggested and displayed. If she has any aspiration for a domain in which she can reign (and for Christian theology the mark of sovereignty is humble service), the borders of that realm come closer to those of art than of science.

It is entirely wholesome for theology to observe the type of unambiguous development of ideas which is open to the empirical sciences and to respect the rigor which is possible for the mathematician. It is not only possible but highly worthwhile for the theologian to seek to produce the same measure of precision and logical certainty *wherever his extensive subject matter and concern permit*—his obligation to communicate with the secular world places before him this responsibility. However, there is the more demanding task of depicting in the richest possible symbolic reference the ultimate concern and meaning of life. For this broader task of creating, criticizing, and transforming those symbols which are most adequate in pointing to meanings which lie beyond literal discourse theology engages in its function as an art. Since her goal is not that of abstract and objective knowledge and her aim not that of producing detached assent, since the certitude which she would present is a certitude which involves the decisions and commitments of men, theology calls upon imagination which is both disciplined and creative. It is as she welcomes and respects this crucial and demanding role that theology finds the realm in which she can both reign and serve.

BIBLIOGRAPHY

BIBLIOGRAPHY

Ayer, A. J., *Language Truth and Logic*. New York: Dover Publications, 1946.

Barth, Karl, *The Doctrine of the Word of God, Church Dogmatics*, Vol. 1. New York: Charles Scribner's Sons, 1936.

Brinton, Crane, *Ideas and Men, the Story of Western Thought*. New York: Prentice-Hall, 1950.

Brunner, Emil, *The Christian Doctrine of God, Dogmatics*, Vol. 1. Philadelphia: The Westminster Press, 1950.

Brunner, Emil, *The Divine Imperative*. Philadelphia: The Westminster Press, 1947.

Brunner, Emil, *Revelation and Reason*. Philadelphia: The Westminster Press, 1946.

Casserley, J. V. L., *The Christian in Philosophy*. New York: Charles Scribner's Sons, 1951.

Casserley, J. V. L., *Graceful Reason, the Contribution of Reason to Theology*. Greenwich, Conn.: Seabury Press, 1954.

Cassirer, Ernst, *Language and Myth*, Susanne K. Langer, translator. New York: Harper & Brothers, 1946.

Collingwood, R. G., *An Essay on Philosophical Method*. New York: Oxford University Press, 1933.

Conant, James B., *Science and Common Sense*. New Haven: Yale University Press, 1951.

Cullmann, Oscar, *Christ and Time*. Philadelphia: The Westminster Press, 1950.

Dewey, John, *A Common Faith*. New Haven: Yale University Press, 1934.

Dewey, John, *The Quest for Certainty, A Study of the Relation of Knowledge and Action*. New York: Minton, Balch & Co., 1929.

DeWolf, L. H., *The Religious Revolt Against Reason*. New York: Harper & Brothers, 1949.

DeWolf, L. H., *A Theology of the Living Church*. New York: Harper & Brothers, 1953.

Ferré, Nels F. S., *Faith and Reason*. New York: Harper & Brothers, 1946.

Fitch, F. B., *Symbolic Logic*. New York: Ronald Press Company, 1952.

Heim, Karl, *God Transcendent*. London: Nisbet and Company, 1935.

Heim, Karl, *The Transformation of the Scientific World View*. New York: Harper & Brothers, 1953.

Langer, Susanne K., *Philosophy in a New Key, A Study in the Symbolism of Reason, Rite, and Art*. Cambridge, Mass.: Harvard University Press, 1942.

MacIntosh, D. C., *The Reasonableness of Christianity*. New York: Charles Scribner's Sons, 1925.

MacIntosh, D. C., *Theology as an Empirical Science*. New York: The Macmillan Company, 1919.

Maritain, Jacques, *An Essay on Christian Philosophy*. New York: Philosophical Library, 1955.

Maritain, Jacques, *The Range of Reason*. New York: Charles Scribner's Sons, 1952.

Maritain, Jacques, *Science and Wisdom*. New York: Charles Scribner's Sons, 1940.

Montague, William P., *The Ways of Knowing, or The Methods of Philosophy*. New York: The Macmillan Company, 1925.

Martineau, James, *The Seat of Authority in Religion*. New York: Longmans, Green & Co., Inc., 1905.

Niebuhr, Reinhold, *The Nature and Destiny of Man*. New York: Charles Scribner's Sons, 1946.

Rall, H. F., *Christianity, An Inquiry into Its Nature and Truth*. New York: Charles Scribner's Sons, 1940.

Reichenbach, Hans, *Experience and Prediction*. Chicago: University of Chicago Press, 1929.

Russell, Bertrand, *An Inquiry into Meaning and Truth*. New York: W. W. Norton & Co., 1940.

Russell, Bertrand, *Our Knowledge of the External World*. Chicago: Open Court Publishing Company, 1929.

Russell, Bertrand, *Mysticism and Logic and Other Essays*. New York: Longmans, Green & Co., Inc., 1925.

Sabatier, Auguste, *Religions of Authority and the Religion of the Spirit*. New York: McClure Phillips & Co., 1904.

Santayana, George, *Interpretations of Poetry and Religion*. New York: Charles Scribner's Sons, 1927.

Santayana, George, *Skepticism and Animal Faith*. London: Constable & Co., Ltd., 1923.

Stace, W. T., *The Theory of Knowledge and Existence*. New York: Clarendon Press, Oxford, 1932.

Taylor, A. E., *The Faith of a Moralist*. London: Macmillan and Co., Ltd., 1930.

Tillich, Paul, *Systematic Theology*, Vol. I. Chicago: University of Chicago Press, 1951.

Wheelwright, Philip, *The Burning Fountain, A Study in the Language of Symbolism.* Bloomington: The Indiana University Press, 1954.

White, Morton, ed., *The Age of Analysis.* Boston: Houghton Mifflin Co., 1955.

Whitehead, Alfred North, *Adventures of Ideas.* New York: The Macmillan Company, 1933.

Whitehead, Alfred North, *Essays in Science and Philosophy.* New York: Philosophical Library, 1948.

Whitehead, Alfred North, *Process and Reality.* New York: Humanities Press, 1929.

Whitehead, Alfred North, *Science and the Modern World.* New York: The Macmillan Company, 1925.

Whitehead, Alfred North, *Religion in the Making.* New York: The Macmillan Company, 1950.

NOTES AND ACKNOWLEDGMENTS

NOTES AND ACKNOWLEDGMENTS

Notes on Chapter One

1. The extent to which science must rely upon metaphysical presuppositions and must formulate its basic theories in terms of abstract, nonempirical conceptualizations is discussed at considerable length by Alfred North Whitehead in *Concept of Nature* and *Science and the Modern World*, by Henry Margenau in *The Nature of Physical Reality*, and by W. T. Stace in *The Theory of Knowledge and Existence*. These are only a few of the modern philosophers and scientists who have focused attention upon the fact that the creative constructions of science, the formation of hypotheses, take place in a realm far removed from direct sensory awareness. James B. Conant goes so far as to assert in *Science and Common Sense* (chapters 2, 3) that a distinctive aim of science is the securing of freedom from direct empirical reference, that the measure of scientific accomplishment is its separation from specific incidents of sensory experience.

Although the rational constructions must have some reference to observed phenomena, they are the product of imagination, speculation, and deductive inferences. Each stage of generalization calls for a departure from perceptual reality. Metaphysical system serves both as the bearer of meaning for recorded observations and as the form of speculative outreach which suggests additional observations or experiments.

2. In *Ideas and Men* Crane Brinton distinguishes between the *cumulative* and *noncumulative* ideas which make up the intellectual history of Western culture. He points out that most of the Great Ideas which determine a culture may be colored by scientific information but do not constitute a body of factual data which may be preserved and extended. Each generation may be familiar with the traditional formulations, but no generation inherits these ideas as settled truths which require no further inquiry.

3. This description is not presented as an adequate or universally acceptable definition of theology. It presupposes that we will be thinking in terms of

Christian theology generally and, more specifically, of what is ordinarily classified as *systematic* theology. The work of historical, Biblical, or "natural" theology is considered to be contributory to the broader task of effecting a formulation of truth which takes account of the historical proclamation of the Church, the witness of Scripture, and the evidence of sense and reason available to all men. In connection with the assertion that theology is a product of human activity, it is important to refer to Karl Barth's discussion of "Dogmatics as an Inquiry." (*The Doctrine of the Word of God*, I, 1, 2.) The sense in which theology is designated as seeking truth of "ultimate concern" refers to Paul Tillich's presentation of this theme in the introduction of *Systematic Theology*, Vol. I.

4. Maritain, Jacques, *An Essay on Christian Philosophy*, p. 15. Philosophical Library, 1955. Used by permission.

5. Maritain, Jacques, *Science and Wisdom*, p. 113. Charles Scribner's Sons, 1940. Used by permission.

6. Maritain, Jacques, *An Essay on Christian Philosophy*, pp. 92-93.

"There are, thus, two ways of linking a new conclusion to an already acquired theological conclusion, since there are two ways of making use of a principle of inference. When a major premise is used *insofar as known*, it is the light of the science in virtue of which it was known that permits us to posit the conclusion. But when this major is used *only insofar as believed*, this can no longer hold true. Then it stands rather as a fact that is imposed on us than as a means of conveying evidence; and it is the proper light of the inferior science which takes the initiative toward the conclusion. Thus the truths *seen* by the blessed in the beatific vision are for the theologian principles *believed* not *seen;* and here we have the reason why the conclusions which theology draws therefrom are borne in virtue of the theological light, and not in virtue of the evidence proper to the science of the blessed."

7. DeWolf, L. Harold, *The Religious Revolt Against Reason*, pp. 37-38. Harper & Brothers, 1949. Used by permission.

Brunner speaks to this same apparent inconsistency in acknowledging:

"Revealed knowledge is poles apart from rational knowledge. These two forms of knowledge are as far from each other as heaven is from earth. And yet, in the very act of expressing this sentence, writing it down, and printing it, we have already put in use the whole apparatus of the human reason and of human culture." From *Revelation and Reason*, p. 16, by Emil Brunner. Copyright, 1946, The Westminister Press. Used by permission.

8. Barth, Karl, *The Doctrine of the Word of God* (Church Dogmatics, Vol. 1), p. 28. Charles Scribner's Sons, 1936. Used by permission.

9. From *The Christian Doctrine of God*, Dogmatics, Vol. I, p. 11, by Emil Brunner. Published by The Westminister Press, 1950. Used by permission.

10. From *The Divine Imperative*, p. 50, by Emil Brunner, translated by Olive Wyon. Copyright, 1947, by W. L. Jenkins, The Westminister Press. Used by permission.

11. Barth, *op. cit.*, p. 7.

12. *Ibid.*, pp. 12 ff.

13. *Ibid.*, pp. 1 ff., 51 ff.

14. *Ibid.*, p. 9.

15. Whitehead, Alfred North, *Adventures of Ideas,* p. 207. The Macmillan Company, 1940. Used by permission.

16. "Religious faiths have come under the influence of philosophies that have tried to demonstrate the fixed union of the actual and ideal in ultimate Being. . . . Religion has also been involved in the metaphysics of substance, and has thrown in its lot with acceptance of certain cosmologies. It has found itself fighting a battle and a losing one with science, as if religion were a rival theory about the structure of the natural world." Dewey, John, *The Quest for Certainty,* p. 303. G. P. Putnam's Sons, 1929. Used by permission.

17. MacIntosh, D. C., *Theology as an Empirical Science,* p. 4. The Macmillan Company, 1940. Used by permission.

18. Dewey, John, *op. cit.*, p. 304.

19. In his anthology of twentieth-century philosophy Morton White designates this period of history as *The Age of Analysis.*

20. The term "analytic philosophy" seems to be the preferred designation for this whole movement. Their common feature is their detailed analysis of the meaning of logical propositions and of ordinary discourse. Also, their primary emphasis is not upon the synthetic aspect of knowledge but upon the reductionist function of critical thought.

21. "Like Hume, I divide all genuine propositions into two classes: those which, in his terminology, concern 'relations of ideas,' and those which concern 'matters of fact.' The former class comprises the *a priori* propositions of logic and pure mathematics, and these I allow to be necessary and certain only because they are analytic. That is, I maintain that the reason why these propositions cannot be confuted in experience is that they do not make any assertion about the empirical world, but simply record our determination to use symbols in a certain fashion. Propositions concerning empirical matters of fact, on the other hand, I hold to be hypotheses, which can be probable but never certain. And in giving an account of the method of their validation I claim also to have explained the nature of truth." From *Language Truth and Logic,* p. 31, by A. J. Ayer. Reprinted through permission by Dover Publications, Inc., New York 10, New York. ($1.25)

22. A good example of the manner in which theological concepts may be subjected to rigorous logical analysis is to be found in J. J. C. Smart's article, "The Existence of God," in *New Essays in Philosophical Theology,* Anthony Flew and Alasdair MacIntyre, editors.

G. E. Moore's question as to whether "existence" may be applied as a predicate term makes it highly debatable as to whether $(\exists x)\phi x$ is a properly formed proposition if ϕ is taken to represent "exists." The logical problem comes into sharper focus if we take the cosmological argument for the existence of God and attempt to assert that "there is a Being whose essence necessarily implies His existence." No matter how structured, the representation involves the malformation of asserting the logical necessity of an existential proposition. $\square(\exists x)[\phi x \supset \psi x]$ or $(\exists x)[\phi x \supset \square \psi x]$ are both logical absurdities.

23. Casserley, J. V. L., *The Scope and Variety of Natural Theology*, p. 14. Charles Scribner's Sons, 1951. Used by permission of the author.

24. Hartt, Julian N., "Dialectic, Analysis, and Empirical Generalization in Theology," *Crozer Quarterly*, XXIX, 1. Crozer Theological Seminary, Chester, Pa. Used by permission.

25. "The crucial error of the School of Vienna has been to assume as self-evident that whatever has no meaning *for the scientist* has no meaning *at all.* In this respect logical positivism remains under the yoke of positivistic preju- dice. But, as to science itself and its logical structure, and what has a meaning for the scientist *as such*, the analysis of the School of Vienna is, I believe, generally accurate and well-founded." Maritain, Jacques, *The Range of Rea- son*, p. 6. Charles Scribner's Sons, 1953. Used by permission.

26. "I propose that any form of words that is grammatically significant shall be held to constitute a sentence, and that every indicative sentence, whether it is literally meaningful or not, shall be regarded as expressing a statement. . . . The word, 'proposition,' on the other hand, will be reserved for what is ex- pressed by sentences which are literally meaningful. . . .

"In putting forward the principle of verification as a criterion of meaning, I do not overlook the fact that the word 'meaning' is commonly used in a variety of senses, and I do not wish to deny that in some of these senses a statement may properly be said to be meaningful even though it is neither analytic nor empirically verifiable. I should, however, claim that there was at least one proper use of the word 'meaning' in which it would be incorrect to say that a statement was meaningful unless it satisfied the principle of verifica- tion; and I have, perhaps tendentiously, used the expression 'literal meaning' to distinguish this use from others. . . . Furthermore, I suggest that it is only if it is literally meaningful, in this sense, that a statement can properly be said to be either true or false." (Ayer, *op. cit.*, pp. 8, 15, 16.)

27. *Ibid.*, p. 34.

28. *Ibid.*, pp. 114-115.

29. *Ibid.*, p. 118.

30. It is interesting to note that a number of theologians would share with Ayer the contention that nothing which is properly "Christian revelation" can be regarded as the "imparting of factual information." See Emil Brunner, *Revelation and Reason*, Introduction and Part Two, Section 24.

31. "It is common to find belief in a transcendent god conjoined with belief in an after-life. But, in the form which it usually takes the content of this belief is not a genuine hypothesis. To say that men do not ever die, or that the state of death is merely a state of prolonged insensibility, is indeed to express a significant proposition, though all available evidence goes to show

that it is false. But to say that there is something imperceptible inside a man, which is his soul or his real self, and that it goes on living after he is dead, is to make a metaphysical assertion which has no more factual content than the assertion that there is a transcendent god." (Ayer, *op. cit.*, p. 117.)

32. Karl Barth protests that quite often the historian, educationalist, and philosopher "judge the Church's language about God on principles foreign to it, instead of on its own principles, and thus increase instead of diminishing the harm on account of which the Church needs a critical science." (*The Doctrine of the Word of God*, p. 5.) He proceeds, however, to specify the manner in which this critical task may properly be undertaken in terms of principles peculiar to the Church.

33. Julian Hartt makes the observation that undue preoccupation with methodological concerns may easily result in the reduction of theology to the same trivial activities which consume so much of the energies of contemporary philosophy. He indicates, quite accurately, that theology cannot expect its technical methodological inquiries to provide the meat of religious discourse. "If there is no such knowledge, methodology cannot create it. If there is no such knowledge, then problems of theological methodology will inevitably prove infertile and trivial." (Hartt, *op. cit.*)

34. Holmer, Paul, "Karl Heim and the Sacrifice of Intellect," *The Lutheran Quarterly*, VI, 3. Editorial Council of Lutheran Theological Seminary, Gettysburg, Pa. Used by permission.

35. Casserley, J. V. L., *op. cit.*, p. 29.

36. Holmer, Paul, "Philosophical Criticism and Christology," *The Journal of Religion*, XXXIV, 2. University of Chicago Press. Used by permission.

In his Christological examination Holmer is willing to explore the possibility of a reduction to the terms of analytic philosophy. ". . .it seems to be plausible to forego the metaphysics and use the tools that are at hand. . . . I refer to the tools of modern philosophical analysis. . . . the important thing to remember is that contemporary philosophy is more appropriate to the learning enterprise of our day than is any other philosophy." In his willingness to converse in the limited confines of analysis Holmer may have failed to make certain "metaphysical" assertions about the nature of Christ which most Christians would regard as important. He has, however, undertaken an important task, that of speaking to the contemporary world in its own chosen terms.

37. The examination of the fusion of Palestinian and Hellenistic strains in Christianity has been the subject of a great deal of scholarly writing. The synthesis has been viewed as a "corruption" or a "development" of Christianity, depending upon the point of view of the writer. In this connection it seems to me that Cullmann has made a mistake in trying to divest Christianity of its Greek influences. The concepts of time and eternity in patristic Christianity were undoubtedly different from those of the New Testament Church, and this difference shows the stamp of Hellenistic metaphysics. Those earlier con-

cepts, however, had already been formed on the basis of earlier "Helleniza-tions" and were projected against the background of various pre-scientific metaphysical systems, Babylonian and Persian among others. There is nothing to be served by selecting a particular expression of metaphysical presupposi-tions and making it serve as normative for Christianity in all ages.

38. The "idealistic" philosophies which a few generations ago were looked upon as the natural foe to Christian faith have come with time to be identified with Christianity. The supernatural element in faith found a way of com-municating itself in the speculative terms of idealism to the extent that the older conflict is almost forgotten. On the contemporary scene it is not unusual to find the apologetic of faith couched in the language which was once used in the attack upon traditional belief.

39. Ferré, Nels F. S., *Faith and Reason*, p. 2. Harper & Brothers, 1946. Used by permission.

Notes on Chapter Two

1. Foreman, Kenneth J., "With Sword and Trowel—The Business of Theology," *The Register* of Louisville Presbyterian Theological Seminary, xxxviii, 2. Used by permission.

2. The term "apologetic" is used throughout this section to refer to the general theological enterprise of vindicating the conclusions of constructive theology against criticism. No sharp distinction is made between the criticisms from the secular world and those from within the Christian community.

3. Barth, Karl, *The Doctrine of the Word of God*, pp. 51 ff.

4. *Ibid.*, pp. 79 ff.

It is quite in order to raise the question of whether or not Barth's rather detailed exposition of what he means by "The Word of God" furnishes us with an *applicable* standard by which dogmatics may test the proclamation of the Church. Certainly he makes it clear that "The Word of God" is no concrete entity which dogmatics *has* and can point to. In fairness it should be emphasized that Barth has recognized far more clearly than most theo-logians the necessity for critical theology and that he has indicated a standard of reference which is *intelligible* to those who are a part of the Christian community even though it may be somewhat lacking in the definiteness which is demanded by critics.

5. Tillich, Paul, *Systematic Theology*, Vol. I, p. 13. (Italics mine.) University of Chicago Press, 1951. Used by permission.

6. Barth, *op. cit.*, pp. 5-6.

7. Tillich, *op. cit.*, p. 12.

8. Barth, *op. cit.*, Chap. 1, sec. 3.

9. Casserley, J. V. L., *The Christian in Philosophy*, pp. 31, 32. Charles Scribner's Sons, 1951. Used by permission.

10. It is because of this fact that Karl Barth would seem to be on firm

ground in rejecting the *analogia entis* in favor of the *analogia fidei* as theology's "way of knowing." The former requires that all being, unapprehended as well as apprehended, be brought under categories of universal classification. The latter makes possible the frank acknowledgment of the unique.

11. Ferré, *Faith and Reason*, pp. 113, 121, 130.

12. When we assert that philosophy must venture beyond that which is subject to empirical verification we undertake, of course, to contradict the dictum of analytic philosophy. The restriction of synthetic judgments to those which admit to empirical verification is to equate science and philosophy. When philosophy proposes certain rational possibilities, it need not insist that these constructions be labelled a form of "knowledge." Even though they be designated "imaginary constructions," these ventures of speculation can recommend themselves for acceptance apart from any anticipated direct confirmation of the senses.

13. Increasingly for modern science reliance must be placed on the *interpretation* of representations of phenomena rather than on direct observation. Susanne Langer has written: "The promiscuous collection and tabulation of data have given way to a process of assigning possible meanings, merely supposed real entities, to mathematical terms, working out the logical results, and then staging certain crucial experiments to check the hypothesis against the actual, empirical results. But the facts which are accepted by virtue of these tests are not actually *observed* at all. With the advance of mathematical technique in physics, the tangible results of experiment have become less and less spectacular; on the other hand, their *significance* has grown in inverse proportion. The men in the laboratory have departed so far from the old forms of experimentation—typified by Galileo's weights and Franklin's kite—that they cannot be said to observe the actual objects of their curiosity at all; instead, they are watching index needles, revolving drums, and sensitive plates. . . . Instead of watching the process that interests us, that is to be verified—say, a course of celestial events, or the behavior of such objects as molecules and ether-waves—we really see only the fluctuations of a tiny arrow, the trailing path of a stylus, or the appearance of a speck of light, and *calculate to the 'facts' of our science.* What is directly observed is only a sign of the 'physical fact'; it requires interpretation to yield scientific propositions. Not simply seeing is believing, but *seeing and calculating, seeing and translating.*" Langer, Susanne, *Philosophy in a New Key,* pp. 19, 20. Harvard University Press, 1942. Used by permission.

The extent to which these mathematical conceptualizations are removed from any direct sensory evidence sometimes poses for the scientist a problem in determining to what extent he is justified in treating them as "real." Henry Margenau *(The Nature of Physical Reality)* would guard against loss of scientific reliability by insisting that all such conceptualizations must have a dual tie to empirical observation. They cannot be "insular," constructed apart from observation, or "peninsular," derived from observations but offering no path back to the perceptual plan. So long as these conceptions are derived from perception and "can find their way back" they belong to the proper field of science.

14. Ferré, *op. cit.*, p. 131.

15. John Dewey, among others, stresses the damage which has been done both to religion and to society generally when theology identifies itself with some particular philosophical system. In *The Quest for Certainty* and in *A Common Faith* he calls for religion to reject all such identifications. It is possible, of course, to call attention to the fact that pragmatism is subject to the same fault against which it would warn religion; it has tended to accept uncritically certain epistemological postulates which are simply features of current scientific procedure. This counter criticism, however, does not detract seriously from the common-sense value of the warning. One need not accept Dewey's admonition that religion disassociate itself completely from all empirical and speculative considerations. It is possible to retain an active concern with the problems of science and philosophy without feeling called upon to absolutize some particular formulation or to pronounce finalistic sanction for a structure which has only vehicular significance.

16. DeWolf, L. Harold, *A Theology of the Living Church*, p. 20. Harper & Brothers, 1953. Used by permission.

Notes on Chapter Three

1. Russell, Bertrand, *An Inquiry into Meaning and Truth*, pp. 23-24. W. W. Norton & Co., 1940. Used by permission.

2. Whitehead's famous indictment of the "bifurcation of nature" is directed in part against this false abstraction involved in the destruction of the subject-object relationship. The assumption that it is possible for the investigator to stand somehow "outside" or "above" his own inquiry and conclusions is responsible for no small part of our confused thinking.

"The theory of prehensions is founded upon the doctrine that there are no concrete facts which are merely public, or merely private. The distinction between publicity and privacy is a distinction of reason, and is not a distinction between mutually exclusive concrete facts. The sole concrete facts, in terms of which actualities can be analysed, are prehensions; and every prehension has its public side and its private side. Its public side is constituted by the complex datum prehended; and its private side is constituted by the subjective form through which a private quality is imposed on the public datum. The separations of perceptual fact from emotional fact; and of causal fact from emotional fact, and from perceptual fact; and of perceptual fact, emotional fact, and causal fact, from purposive fact; have constituted a complex of bifurcations, fatal to a satisfactory cosmology." Whitehead, A. N., *Process and Reality*, p. 444. The Macmillan Company, 1933. Used by permission.

3. "Speculative Philosophy is the endeavor to frame a coherent, logical, necessary system of general ideas in terms of which every element of our experience can be interpreted. . . .

" 'Coherence,' as here employed, means that the fundamental ideas, in terms of which the scheme is developed, presuppose each other so that in isolation they are meaningless. This requirement does not mean that they are definable in terms of each other; it means that what is indefinable in one such notion cannot be abstracted from its relevance to the other notions. . . . In other words, it is presupposed that no entity can be conceived in complete abstraction from the system of the universe, and that it is the business of speculative philosophy to exhibit this truth." (*Ibid.*, pp. 4, 5.)

4. "Logic places alternatives before us, but never tells us which alternative we are to choose. You can believe not-R, but if so you cannot believe P. Or you can believe P, but if so you cannot believe not-R. You can believe either P or not-R, but not both. You have your choice between the alternatives (P&R) and (not-P & not-R). But no logic and no reasoning can ever tell you which of these two you ought to believe. This is really saying no more than that the function of deductive reasoning is to guarantee, not truth, but consistency—an old enough doctrine, to be sure." Stace, W. T., *The Theory of Knowledge and Existence*, p. 346. Oxford University Press, 1932. Used by permission.

5. "Methodological assumptions are always assumptions regarding which we have a *choice*. We can choose one method or another. We can make one assumption or its opposite. The results of our choice will be greater or less convenience of working. And that is all." (*Ibid.*, p. 354.)

6. Rall, H. F., *Christianity, An Inquiry into Its Nature and Truth*, p. 251. Charles Scribner's Sons, 1940. Used by permission.

7. Santayana, George, *Skepticism and Animal Faith*, p. 35. Constable & Co., Ltd. Used by permission.

8. Reichenbach contends that there are a class of "super-empirical" statements which have a meaning derived from their bearing upon decision regarding lines of action. Concepts concerning the nature of God and of life after death call for particular responses consistent with them. "The statement of life after death involves future experiences similar to those we have in ordinary life; if we must contest its physical truth meaning, we cannot deny its logical meaning. Such statements may become bases of action if they are supposed to be true; for, if a statement is to become a basis of action, it is sufficient if we think it to be true." Reichenbach, Hans, *Experience and Prediction*, p. 65. University of Chicago Press. Copyright 1929 by the University of Chicago. Used by permission.

9. *Ibid.*, p. 393.

10. Paul Holmer in an article, "The Nature of Religious Propositions," *The Review of Religion*, March, 1955, explores at some length the criticisms of analytic philosophy. Rejecting the restrictions which would dump all religious

affirmations into a heap called "meaningless," he contends that there are "truths about possibilities." These, too, are meaningful and with them religion proposes to deal.

11. There is a special problem connected with the question of whether or not contradictory affirmations may be endured within the formulations of theology. This is to be discussed later in the chapter in connection with the place of *paradox* in theological construction.

12. James Martineau in *The Seat of Authority in Religion* examines the various specifications of authority for religious inquiry but assumes that the distinctive feature of religion is that it accords uncritical allegiance to some objective norm.

13. "The chief reason for the continuance of authoritarianism as a method lies not in its logical but in its psychological appeal. Men who are intellectually lazy or timid will always welcome the appeal to cease thinking for themselves and to believe what they are told to believe. Such men enjoy the freedom from responsibility which their conformity brings. So far from being ashamed of accepting a doctrine on the mere say-so of someone else, they actually make a virtue out of their weakness, and singing the praises of blind faith, they proceed to persecute those who seek truth for themselves. . . .

"We should, however, be on our guard against two possible misunderstandings of the position here set forth. First, the refusal to accept an authoritarian defense of a doctrine is by no means a refusal to accept the doctrine itself. The fact that the premises adduced in support of a conclusion are false is no indication that the conclusion is false. . . . The second possible misunderstanding against which we should guard is that in rejecting authority as a primary sanction, we should by no means reject it as a secondary source of knowledge." Montague, Wm. P., *The Ways of Knowing*, pp. 48, 49. The Macmillan Company, 1925. Used by permission.

14. "The newspapers, at one time, said that I was dead, but after carefully examining the evidence I came to the conclusion that the statement was false." (Russell, *op. cit.*, p. 97.)

15. Contemporary theologians are far less concerned than were those of a few generations ago to argue for the sole authority of some single objective standard. The recognized unity of the two Covenants of Scripture, of the early Church, of the continuing Church, of the inner working of the Holy Spirit, far outweighs the importance of seeking to make one of these completely normative for the others.

16. Auguste Sabatier's *Religions of Authority and the Religion of the Spirit* is a protest not against authority as such but against externalized and objectified authority. Religion must concern itself with more than the inventions and discoveries of men. It is a binding of self to something which has originated beyond the self but has been genuinely appropriated.

17. Taylor, A. E., *The Faith of a Moralist*, Vol. II, pp. 231, 232. The Macmillan Company, 1930. Used by permission.

18. Whitehead, A. N., *Religion in the Making*, p. 123. The Macmillan Company, 1950. Used by permission.

19. Collingwood, R. G., *An Essay on Philosophical Method*, pp. 1, 174. Oxford University Press, 1933. Used by permission.

20. The bulk of theological construction consists in the effort to present certain basic Christian concepts and commitments in propositional form, to draw necessary inferences from those general propositions, and to discredit those statements which would be inconsistent with the propositions as formulated. This is an essentially rational exercise.

When we make the assertion, "It is through the death and resurrection of Jesus Christ that the salvation of men is accomplished," our assertion has rational as well as existential content. The pronouncement, "If you trust in God's redeeming act, you will inherit eternal life," is not only a hortatory utterance but also a logical proposition which constitutes a part of a chain of deductive inferences. The manner in which we draw such inferences can claim no independence from the laws of valid thought. Thus, if we venture to say, "Every man who trusts in Christ will be saved; this man believes and therefore will be saved," the truth rests alike upon a reference to the truth of the general Christian conviction and upon the validity of the logical construction $[(\chi)[\phi\chi\supset\Psi\chi] \ \& \ \phi a] \supset \Psi a$. Similarly, the conclusion, "This man who does not believe will not be saved," may also be true. It is not inconsistent so far as rational content is concerned. It cannot, however, be asserted upon the strength of the faulty construction $[(\chi)[\phi\chi\supset\Psi\chi] \ \& \sim \phi b] \supset \sim \Psi b$.

One of the basic problems resides in the question of whether or not the truths which make up the Christian commitment can be reduced to or expressed in genuine propositional form. If this cannot be done, then the whole procedure is lacking in rational soundness.

21. The question of the propositional character of religious utterances has been subjected to considerable examination in contemporary thought. Much of this examination is of technical nature and turns upon the problem of the possibility of equating an idea and a linguistic form. The special relevance for theology does not rest upon these technical considerations, however. Both Barth and Brunner have served to clarify the matter in their examination of the content of revelation. The denial of the propriety of equating the "Word of God" with any static or objective "thing" (Barth) and the insistence that what is communicated in revelation is of the order of "person" rather than "fact" (Brunner and others) serve to correct the assumption that Christian truth is a set of propositions. To acknowledge that propositional forms must be employed for the sake of systematic formulation is one thing; to accept them as strict logical propositions is quite another thing.

22. The antinomian heresies from Marcion to Rasputin are simply chains of reasoning based upon the employment of "salvation is a gift" as a major premise. The Christological heresies from the first century on arise from treating as a logical proposition the assertion "Christ is God" or "Christ is a

real human." The universalist heterodoxies all come from the seemingly valid implications necessitated by taking "God is good" to be a proposition of univocal reference.

23. Brunner, Emil, *The Christian Doctrine of God,* p. 76.

24. Milton, John, *Paradise Lost,* Book I, lines 25-26.

25. Frederic Brenton Fitch—*Symbolic Logic.* Copyright 1952 The Ronald Press Company. Used by permission.

26. Susanne K. Langer in *Philosophy in a New Key,* chapter 1, calls attention to the tendency of exhausted philosophical systems to degenerate into idle fascination with questions which permit of multiple answers, none of which can claim anything other than temperamental sanction.

27. If we take for an example the affirmation, "Jesus Christ was the Word of God incarnate in human flesh," the form of statement enables us to deal with it as a logical proposition. The subject matter, however, warns that extreme caution must be preserved in assuming its propositional character. The question arises as to whether all its component parts can be taken as having unambiguous meaning; whether "Word of God," for instance, has a definable reference. Treated as a proposition this affirmation has served as the basis for the inference, "Jesus was omniscient"; also for the inference, "Jesus was not omniscient." The contradiction highlighted in the inferences is, of course, present in the affirmation from which they are drawn. It would be difficult to imagine any system of rational procedure which enabled one to treat as propositional an utterance which contains an inconsistency within itself. It is possible to maintain that the truth of the initial affirmation simply is not properly expressed. This may well be the case. The difficulty resides in finding some alternative expression which avoids the objectionable feature.

28. Rall, H. F., *op. cit.,* p. 68.

29. MacIntosh, D. C., *Theology as an Empirical Science,* p. 11. The Macmillan Company, 1919. Used by permission.

30. MacIntosh, D. C., *The Reasonableness of Christianity,* p. 243. Charles Scribner's Sons, 1925. Used by permission.

31. The language in which the more general religious experiences are recounted relies almost entirely upon figures of speech borrowed from the empirical realm. One tells of *hearing* the voice of God, of *seeing* His glory. Even the more ambiguous term of *feeling* ("feeling the presence of God, feeling His love") is borrowed from the tactile experience. The more extreme mystic will insist that his insights are based upon a form of awareness which, though at least as compelling, is not identical with that of the physical senses. In communicating his awareness, however, he finds it necessary to rely upon description in terms of physical sensation.

32. Russell, Bertrand, *Our Knowledge of the External World,* pp. 21, 22, 25. Cf. Reichenbach, *op. cit.,* pp. 5, 6, 7. "The psychological operations of thinking are rather vague and fluctuating processes; they almost never keep to the

ways prescribed by logic and may even skip whole groups of operations which would be needed for a complete exposition of the subject in question. . . .

"The way, for instance, in which a mathematician publishes a new demonstration, or a physicist his logical reasoning in the foundation of a new theory, would almost correspond to our concept of rational reconstruction; and the well-known difference between the thinker's way of finding this theorem and his way of presenting it before a public may illustrate this difference in question. I shall introduce the terms *context of discovery* and *context of justification* to mark this distinction."

33. "In Old Testament times prophets were classified as true or false according as their religious inspirations were objectively validated or not. In New Testament times the greatest apostle insisted that God was not the author of confusion, even when it came in connection with religious experience, and that inspirations should be tested, to prove whether or not they were from God." (MacIntosh, *Theology as an Empirical Science*, p. 33.)

34. The justification of a belief, controverted by evidence of one order, in terms of evidence of some other order is discussed in the section of this chapter dealing with "Convergence as the Integrating Method of Theology."

35. "Revelation is understood as something objective, as something which confronts us, as something outside ourselves. But this is a very improper and inexact way of speaking; for revelation is certainly not a 'something,' a 'thing'; but it is a process, an event, and indeed an event which happens to us and in us." (Brunner, *The Christian Doctrine of God*, p. 19.)

36. "As many minds as there are that know him at first hand, so many revealing acts have there been; and as many as know him only at second hand are strangers to revelation: they may hold, or think they hold, what has been revealed to another; but, in passing through media to them, it has become Natural religion." Martineau, James, *The Seat of Authority in Religion*, p. 337. Longmans, Green & Co., Inc., 1905.

37. The term "hairetic" does not appear in the English dictionary. It is here employed to designate the quality of *choice* or *selection* in the formation of a judgment. Derived from the Greek αἱρετίζω, and in turn from αἱρῶ, it calls attention to the act of "taking on one's self."

The familiar English word "heretic" is, of course, identical in its derivation. It has become colored by the general notion that any decision which is made on the basis of individual preference *as opposed to the catholicity of view* constitutes heterodoxy. That which one decides for himself is therefore viewed with suspicion or disfavor.

In preserving a spelling closer to the Greek root the effort is being made to use a word which keeps the sense of the original without taking on the derived coloration. The act of making personal decision is not in and of itself an act of either conformity or non-conformity. It is, rather, the inescapable element in every determination of an individual either to conform or not to conform with reference to a prevailing opinion.

38. "Scientific method is not, in every step of its procedure, directed by the principle of validity; there are other steps which have the character of volitional decisions. It is this distinction which we must emphasize at the very beginning of epistemological investigations. That the idea of truth, or validity, has a directive influence in scientific thinking is obvious and has at all times been noticed by epistemologists. That there are certain elements of knowledge, however, which are not governed by the idea of truth, but which are due to volitional resolutions, and though highly influencing the makeup of the whole system of knowledge, do not touch its truth-character, is less known to philosophical investigators. The presentation of the volitional decisions contained in the system of knowledge constitutes, therefore, an integral part of the critical task of epistemology. . . . To find out all the points at which decisions are involved is one of the most important tasks of epistemology." (Reichenbach, *op. cit.*, p. 9.)

39. Whitehead, A. N., *Adventures of Ideas*, p. 313.

40. Santayana, George, *Interpretations of Poetry and Religion*, p. 7. Charles Scribner's Sons, 1927. Used by permission.

41. The presupposition of order, whether it takes the form of "the uniformity of nature" or "the principle of causality," stands as necessary only in the sense that *it is necessary for further investigation.*

42. Tillich, Paul, *Systematic Theology*, Vol. I, p. 60.

43. Rall, H. F., *op. cit.*, p. 145.

44. MacIntosh, D. C., *The Reasonableness of Christianity*, p. 167.

45. DeWolf, L. H., *A Theology of the Living Church*, p. 28.

46. Reichenbach, Hans, *op. cit.*, p. 396.

47. Santayana, George, *Skepticism and Animal Faith*, p. v.

48. Tillich, Paul, *op. cit.*, p. 60.

Notes on Chapter Four

1. Whitehead, A. N., *Adventures of Ideas*, pp. 206, 221.

2. Reichenbach, Hans, *Experience and Prediction*, pp. 16, 17.

3. Barth, Karl, *The Doctrine of the Word of God*, ch. 1, sec. 3.

4. The incidents are manifold and ludicrous of treating non-propositional theological utterances as if they constituted logical propositions which could serve as elements of a syllogism. These range all the way from deducing sociological requirements from the masculinity of God (the Scriptures use the masculine pronoun) to a calculation of the population of heaven from the cubic measurements of the holy city given in the Apocalypse.

5. The meaningful poetic language of an agrarian culture may be lost completely on members of an industrial community. Similarly, the appropri-

ation of a first-century Semitic metaphor by twentieth-century Western thought experiences further reinterpretation before it can carry its original force in Far Eastern missions.

6. Langer, Susanne K., *Philosophy in a New Key* (Harvard University Press, 1942), and Wheelwright, Philip, *The Burning Fountain* (The Indiana University Press, 1954).

7. A. N. Whitehead finds it important to treat God as an element in a categorial scheme of existence as well as in the scheme of explanation. This meets a requirement of philosophy but does not coincide with the approach of theology. Tillich's unwillingness, on the other hand, to ascribe "existence" to God is an expression of this awareness of uniqueness. None of the categories of description, even that of existence, can be applied. To treat God as a member of a class, even the class of existing beings, may be necessary for discourse, but it involves a qualification of His uniqueness.

8. Santayana, George, *Skepticism and Animal Faith*, p. 7.

9. Dewey, John, *The Quest for Certainty*, p. 308.

Notes on Chapter Five

1. Semanticists seek to define *symbols* as representation of entities or ideas by means of acts, sounds, or objects which have no essential connection with that which is represented. Through some type of mutual agreement the symbol serves to call to mind some concept or reality not a part of the immediate sensory environment. *Signs* are units or elements of sensory experience which come to represent other elements with which they have been observed to have some sort of direct connection.

2. "It has frequently been noted that the intellectual link between language and myth is metaphor; but in the precise definition of the process, and even in regard to the general direction it is supposed to take, theories are widely at variance. . . .

"Indeed, even the most primitive verbal utterance requires a transmutation of a certain cognitive or emotive experience into sound, i.e., into a medium that is foreign to the experience, and even quite disparate; just as the simplest mythical form can arise only by virtue of a transformation which removes a certain impression from the realm of the ordinary, the everyday and profane, and lifts it to the level of the 'holy,' the sphere of the mythico-religious 'significance.' This involves not merely a transference, but a real μετάβασις ἐις ἄλλο γένος; in fact, it is not only a transition to another category, but actually the creation of the category itself." Cassirer, Ernst, *Language and Myth*, pp. 84, 87-88. Harper & Brothers, 1946. Used by permission.

3. The homiletic distortions of the parables of Jesus, the literalism with which His figures of speech are sometimes interpreted, has led to the sort of

Whitworth College Library
Spokane, Washington

thinking which would take His admonition that we be "as doves" to mean that we should grow feathers and lay eggs.

4. The person who brings to the Scriptures certain pacifist inclinations will take quite literally the admonitions regarding the "other cheek" and the "second mile," while interpreting figuratively any reference to Jesus' coming to bring "not peace but a sword." The person with opposing convictions will simply reverse the approach to the different passages. Interestingly enough, the person who wishes to regard the Song of Solomon in the most allegorical manner may choose to look upon Jonah most literally, while the person who rejects allegorical use of the Song of Solomon may take Jonah as purely figurative in significance.

5. There is a marked tendency to accept the mixing of traditional symbols much more readily than the introduction of new metaphors. There may be a literary, but not a religious, protest against the fusion of the figures of speech: "Rock of Ages, cleft for me . . . Let the water and the blood, From Thy wounded side which flowed . . ." In spite of changing means of transportation there is a tendency to hold to the figure of the pilot of a ship; "Jesus, Saviour, pilot me Over life's tempestuous sea"; but to feel a bit suspicious of the affirmation, "Jesus is my airplane pilot." Similarly, even in a changing political setting the metaphor of "King" remains acceptable where the word "President" is felt to be inadequate.

6. Both Cassirer and Pepper call attention to the "root metaphor" which appears in all forms of systematic discourse. With reference to the employment of the metaphor of person in the realm of religion Cassirer observes: "This step [to monotheism] is accomplished as soon as the unity which so far has been sought through the objective world, and expressed in objective terms, is turned into a subjective essence, and the meaning of divinity is approached not through the existence of things, but through the being of the Person, the Self. . . . When God, revealing himself to Moses, is asked what name Moses should bear to the Israelites, in case they want to know what god has sent him to them, the answer is: 'I am that I am. Thus thou shalt say to them: I am has sent me unto you.' It is only by this transformation of objective existence into subjective being that the Deity is really elevated to the 'absolute' realm, to a state that cannot be expressed through any analogy with things or names of things. The only instruments of speech that remain for its expression are the personal pronouns: 'I am he; I am the first, the last,' as it is written in the Prophetic Books." (Cassirer, *op. cit.*, pp. 76-77.)

7. Logicians are not in full agreement on the way in which this concept is best represented. The simplest notion is that contained in the operational rule which permits the disjunction p v -p to follow directly from p.

8. The phrase "this book" serves as the symbol for an object, but the symbol is not required if the book can be used as its own reference. When the particular object in question is not a part of the immediate sensory environment, the symbol provides a means of making it an object of cognition. In

the case of abstractions, however, one symbol may be used to explain another, but some act of symbolic transformation is required.

9. We may employ a method of analogy quite accurately in discussing the state of affairs of the moon. We can, for instance, say that it is similar to but not identical with the earth, specifying the quantitive differences of mass, velocity, and relative position. Because of the quantitive comparisons, conclusions may be drawn regarding such matters as the presence or absence of an atmosphere. Simply to say that the moon is smaller than the earth does not provide any basis for concluding that it has no atmosphere; some strict basis of comparison must exist. To contend that God is "like, but not exactly like" human beings or other objects of experience suggests certain meaningful concepts but permits no specific logical inferences unless the nature and degree of likeness can be precisely indicated.

10. Barth, Karl, *The Doctrine of the Word of God*, p. 2.

11. Whitehead, A. N., *Adventures of Ideas*, p. 313.

INDEX